DIARY OF A
DEPLORABLE!

DIARY OF A DEPLORABLE!

A Christian Perspective On Today's Headlines

Dr. William N. Bender, Deplorable

ARPress
ILLUMINATING IDEAS
EMPOWERING VOICES

ARPress
45 Dan Road Suite 5
Canton, MA 02021

Hotline: 1(888) 821-0229
Fax: 1(508) 545-7580

Ordering Information: You may order this book at Curraheebook.com

Quantity sales. Special discounts are available on quantity purchases by corporations, associations, and others. For details, contact the publisher at the address above.

Printed in the United States of America.

ISBN-13:   Softcover   979-8-89356-075-6
              eBook   979-8-89356-076-3

Library of Congress Control Number: 2024904019

TABLE OF CONTENTS

Diary of a Deplorable
Christian Reflections by a Cancelled Conservative

William N. Bender, Ph.D.
Benderbilly53@gmail.com

INTRODUCTION

Love, joy, peace, patience, kindness, goodness, faithfulness, gentleness, and self-control (Galatians, 5: 22 - 24). I pray I demonstrate each of these as I write this book. I like to laugh, but these topics are challenging, and emotions run high. Thus, reflections on these issues, will require all of these Gifts of the Spirit. I pray Christians will wake up, and begin to speak against evil, in all it's many forms. Jesus did! If this requires us to be politically incorrect, then so be it. Let's use humor, prayer, and truth to begin to stop the evil represented in today's headlines. May God protect us, and lead us in this work!

I am a retired white professor, an old hippie that morphed into a libertarian, and ultimately into a Christian conservative. I am also an avid believer in American Exceptionalism and the American experiment in self-government. As a conservative, I was at one point a victim of the cancel culture—all of the left leaning, politically woke dishonesties, the outright lies, the distorted narratives and half-truths, the rumor campaigns, and the destructive identity politics of the left. I was a politically active conservative in a liberal university setting, and that was enough to really piss off a number of gay folks. I note this because, having been a cancelled victim of the dishonest left, and as a conservative, Christian, white male, I am now highly vested in this struggle against dishonesty, cancellation, and the destructive identity politics of wokeness.

To the woke left: I believe in you. I also believe in Bigfoot, so don't get too excited.

In particular, I see that in 2023, this problem as getting much, much worse. Every day the news headlines demonstrate that dishonest "woke" attacks of this nature have increased against Christians, against whites, against conservatives, against Catholics, and against all males and all Republicans, and even against country music performers and professional racing drivers whose political tweets are objectionable to the woke nazis on the left. Today one can be cancelled by overt lies, and anti-white discrimination just for writing a non-racist country song or liking a funny tweet. You can find these attacks every day in the national headlines, and in all honesty, you probably picked up this diary because you feel the same. You may have been attacked yourself by wokeness in some form or another. Attacks are standard strategy against anyone and everyone with conservative views, and once an allegation is made, it is viewed as "proven" by the woke left. In their view, all Christian conservatives and all republicans are "deplorables."

Let's embrace the term, deplorable! The woke left is going to hate conservative Christians anyway, so let's let them. We'll use honesty, fact-based arguments, Jesus' example of love, and humor to disarm them.

Some may believe that ignoring the insanities of ideologies like the lies of Joe Biden, of Black Lives Matter, of the "trans" community, of Critical Race Theory, or radical leftist political wokeism may be more appropriate than giving these issues any attention at all. However, these lies and attacks do hurt people, sometimes suspending or ending their profession. In many, if not most cases those victims of the woke left are basically innocent of racism, sexism, homophobic hatred, or whatever they are accused of. Thus, the real harm of these woke attacks is the harm they ultimately do to our society as a whole. Such woke attacks are often intended to stifle debate, or even stifle opinions with which the leftists disagree. In that sense, these dishonest attacks are a threat to our national way of life, and to the free expression of ideas on which public debate should be founded.

While there is power in the uniqueness of the American experiment in self-government, there is nothing inevitable about the success of this American dream. Our freedoms can easily be lost by ignoring real ideological threats to America, including threats that are based in lies and half-truths such as these ideologies from the woke left today.

One need only reflect that the hatred inherent within Hitler's Germany developed in one of the most highly educated nations on earth in the 1930s. That nazi hatred was a cancer that brought the entire world to war and it succeeded for a time, simply because good honest people in Germany did not speak out against those hatreds in the early years of the 1930s. Further, one has to note that many of the tactics used by the radical left today are exactly the same as those used by Hitler—elimination of free speech, attempting to disarm political rivals, and terrorizing anyone who disagrees with the proposed ideology, in this case the beliefs of the woke left. The left routinely uses such "shaming" in an effort to silence all opponents, just as Hitler did. Thus, I do see a real need today to oppose these woke ideas that may, over time, destroy America.

In short, let's dive right in!

I went swimming today and took a pee in the deep end. Lifeguard blew his whistle so loud I almost fell in!

For that reason, I believe that someone like myself, should respond to some of the politically woke dishonesties that seem to be infesting our culture like a deadly virus. I've already been cancelled after all, and other than a bit of name calling, not much can be done to injure me or my family any longer. I'm just not that important. However, our American experiment is, and our very way of life does seem to be in jeopardy from the radical left today, unless caring Americans do respond to these attacks and the dumb ideas fostered today by the woke left. Today, more and more Americans are *realizing this. One need only read a bit about growing opposition to critical race theory, or note the "fall" in attendance of the politically "woke" Disney theme parks, the lack of box office draw of various "woke" movies, not to mention the anti-Bud Light beer campaign, to see that many citizens are fed up with wokeness. So I have to ask myself, how should a deplorable, white male, conservative Christian respond?*

At this point, I should probably mention that as a professor, I've written 52 books in my life, and as that fact may indicate, I generally think issues through most completely when I write about them. I usually take on serious topics using some humor, so on this holiday, July 4, 2023, in pondering the poor state of our fragile, weak nation, along with the attacks on Christians, Republicans, whites, conservatives, and other "deplorables" like myself, I have decided to put a few thoughts on paper, a diary, if you will, in which I'll use headlines, truth, biblical principles and humor to confront these woke lies. Further, I intend to dedicate my remaining years to a singular cause—an effort to save America from itself—specifically, from the political left which seems to be so engaged in destroying our nation, just as they once tried to destroy me.

With this in mind, I offer a few reflections that will deal with most of today's major headlines, and I intend to offer a Conservative, Christian perspective on these matters, while proudly presenting and defending American Exceptionalism, and the ever-attainable American Dream. This is not a response to being attacked. Rather, this a much more important book; it is an effort to speak truth in America today, a country in which speaking the truth can get anyone cancelled. I'm not worried about being cancelled—I already have been! Thus, my freedom to speak the truth to the woke, liberal democratic leftists.

And you will know the truth, and the truth shall set you free (John 8: 32)

The issue here is the hatred, the dishonesty, and the ongoing threat to America and our society today by the neo-Nazis of the woke left, and the promoters of self-selected victimization. The truth is, those ideologues are guilty of virtually everything they accuse we deplorables of. When those ideologues attempt to cancel anyone expressing a different opinion, they attempt to cancel the fundamental right of free speech in America. And America, like all republics is dependent on honest exchanges of ideas. I will no longer tolerate being silenced. What I do promise is that this diary will hold nothing back. If an idea is really bad, only half-true, thoroughly dishonest, or unusually destructive, I will so label it. Given the childish, rather snowflake tendency of many on the woke left to be offended by virtually everything, I'm sure this diary will offend many people. If this is published I'll again be called racist, sexist, neo- nazi, or whatever. Of course, being a deplorable conservative Christian, I'm already called those things, as are most of you.

No doubt some people will be offended by this book! However, giving offense is not my intention here. As I stated above, my intention is to provide a conservative, Christian response to some of the really dumb things happening in our society, with particular attention to things that may, over time, end American society as we know it.

Still, preparing this response should be great fun, as well as thought provoking. Also, I like to use humor when I write, because humor disarms ideologues of whatever stripe. Thus, among these reflections, I'll toss in a few memes, just for fun. This should help keep this diary a bit more light, even though this is truly serious stuff.

Finally, I invite like-minded folks to join me in this endeavor. Share this diary with others as you like, and contact me with your thoughts. I'll respond as I can. Again, I hope that these reflections will present a coherent, thoughtful juxtaposition to much of the leftist thought in the headlines. Now, let's let the fun begin!

Note: This Diary now circulates in five states, as conservative Christians share it with others. Please do more of that! Forward this along to anyone on your email list, and maybe over time, we can change a few things. The

Diary is shared today in Georgia, North and South Carolina, Louisiana, and Texas. If you like I can add your name or anyone's email to the email distribution list (which typically gets four to six pages of these reflections every couple of weeks), or you can simply send this along it to others. Please, please, don't be silent any longer. To ignore evil dishonesty, is to perpetuate evil dishonesty. Hopefully this Diary can help refute such dishonesty. At a minimum this will make your friends think, and hopefully laugh a bit.

REFLECTION 1:

Democrats And The Biden Crime Family

(initially written 7/4/2023)

I've been personally attacked before, and because these attacks of the woke left seem to be getting more common, I am now highly vested in this struggle. I believe that as conservatives, we all need to immediately form Committees of Correspondence, much as our forefathers did in the 1770s. Further, we need to do it for the same reason—our government is strangling us to death! We must remember that the British in 1775 wished to shut down any dissenting opinion other than the government's views. They wanted to tax citizens to death, and take citizen's guns! Does this sound familiar? The fight at Lexington and Concord Bridge involved a British expedition to capture arms stored in Lexington after all! All of these same things are happening today, driven by the woke ideologies of the left. Here are a few more particulars on our government stealing our freedoms, straight from the headlines.

This week a federal judge stated in a formal, though temporary decision, that President Biden has abridged my first amendment right to free speech. As stated by this Judge, the Biden administration has "probably" violated the US Constitution by colluding with big tech to censor free speech of Christians and conservatives. Numerous examples were cited ranging from differing opinions on the Covid outbreak, to outright government lying about the Hunter Biden laptop computer, emails from which show *our current president to be a criminal! These government actions designed to silence political opposition are the kind of stuff one might expect in Russia or North Korea, and this I will not tolerate. No man will take away my right of free expression, and this includes Mr. Biden and his criminal cronies. I choose not to listen to the dishonesties of slow joe and his cronies anymore.*

Wify told me to get the spider out of the bathtub, but not kill him. She wanted me to take him out, so I took him out. We had a few drinks; Nice guy overall; he's a web designer. Now who says I don't listen to her???

However, as a Christian deplorable, many other things presently disturb me about our federal government. I do not want my tax dollars used for abortions, yet I'm forced to fund Planned Parenthood—a not-to-subtle abortion mill-- with my tax dollars. This is unchristian. I also do not want my taxes used to suborn the US Constitution, yet our federal government, under President Joe Biden, seems determined to restrict our constitutional right to bear arms. He swore to uphold that right, along with my first amendment right to free speech, when he swore to uphold the US Constitution, but he has violated that oath, and it seems that sacred oaths matter little to him. The same president, and it seems almost all democrats, seem determined to undermine the American family, the backbone of our nation, through such actions as "gender surgery for minors" without either parental consent or notification. I also note that the newly weaponized fbi (please note the disrespect I have for that corrupt political organization, as represented by the lower-case letters!) now views parents at PTA meetings, and all Catholics as "terrorists!" At times it seems that the whole "queer/ transgender" movement is determined to destroy our families. Remember that "transgenders" at a "pride" parade recently chanted, "We are coming for your children." I see every reason to believe them, and the democrats seem to support this horrid movement completely, along with Biden's other illegal moves.

Further, the democrats seem determined to weaken America in general in many ways, destroying our economy via increased gas prices, food prices, and taxation, and ignoring the crisis at our border with Mexico. Biden has damaged us greatly in forbidding the use of fossil fuels. I have to note Biden said he would "end fossil fuels" when he ran for office, and he is doing so in America with his every action, from prohibitions on natural gas stoves, to restrictions on oil leases. Of course, while doing that, he is begging other nations to produce and export MORE oil to the US. Thus, he is not moving toward a clean environment, as he likes to claim. Rather, he is merely ending fossil fuel production exclusively in the USA while also killing our economy, while at the same time, he is encouraging more fossil fuel development elsewhere. This means that we are sending more US dollars overseas to pay for it! This cannot possibly make logical sense to anyone, but then again if you watch Biden closely, any honest person can see his dementia almost daily in the news. Should we really expect this demented president to make sense? As an example of his disjointed thoughts, he said last week that the American economy was strong! With groceries and gas prices going through the roof, does that make sense to anyone?

Definition: Deja Poo The feeling that I've heard this crap before!

Anyone reading a newspaper or following an online news feed (other than CNN or the New York Times, of course) has to admit that Biden and the democrats have used almost every federal agency as a weapon against the American people—essentially against you and me. The irs (whose agents now are packing guns, for the first time in US history!), the fbi, the departments of injustice and homeland insecurity, all are targeting Americans who disagree with the liberal "Woke" agenda. Representative Jim Jordan, a Conservative Congressman whom I respect greatly, recently made this same point. Christians and traditional conservative Americans are now the main targets of this government for various investigations. Why should I support a government who has declared me as their enemy?

The older I get the more I understand why roosters just scream when they start their day.

While impeaching President Trump twice, and filing uncounted charges against him in court—none of which have been proven true--the democratic powers that be seem incapable of investigating the Hunter Biden/ joe Biden influence peddling scheme, or the millions of dollars the Biden family earned from China and other countries, by selling "influence." Why? Why can democrats make up imaginary charges against Trump and ignore serious illegalities by Biden? At this point our nation is run, not by a freely elected government, but by the Biden crime family, the most influential crime family in history, as Newt Gingrich recently stated. Further these criminals are supported by the democratic party.

I wrote about these issues to my two Senators from Georgia, both of whom are democrats. Neither responded to my points on these issues, thus showing a complete lack of integrity on their part. This dumb dishonesty is what one should expect from democrats today.

I think of democrats and it just makes me wonder; are you really the sperm that won?

This Biden crime family weakens America at a very dangerous time in history, and our enemies have taken note. I have to mention here that many in our military, while forced to push the leftist "woke" agenda on military personnel, are also proclaiming that we will be at war with China by 2025. Unfortunately, the military is more worried about correct "pronoun usage" along with renaming military bases to appease the woke left, than about preparing for a war which they believe is coming! That should be a serious wake up call to all Americans, but few have noticed. At this rate, we should prepare to learn Mandarin Chinese in a few short years.

Still, as a thinking man, I do not believe that this war with China is really going to emerge, and here is my singular reason; with this weak, demented president in power, China will not need to go to war with us. They can win by waiting! China can merely buy up all our farmland (as they are doing already) to control the food supply, and then wait until America bankrupts itself by refusing to use our own natural fossil fuel abundance.

We are the only nation in history to refuse to use our own natural resources to help build our nation. We keep our oil locked up in our "Strategic Reserve" while we pay for oil overseas. China already owns our national debt, and if Biden gets his way, they will soon own more of it as our budget deficit increases. For this reason, important nations around the world are abandoning the US dollar (specifically Brazil, China, Russia, Italy, etc.). Our nation grows weaker and weaker with this weakness of the dollar. When Biden took office, the dollar was the world currency standard; today nations are abandoning it. With this president and this democratic party holding any power in Washington, these trends will continue, and if they do, our nation is doomed.

It is time to take action and begin to save America, and only conservative citizens like you and me can do it. All persons of like mind are welcome to join in this effort. Historically the Committees of Correspondence served as meeting forums, and clearing houses for information from one American colony to another. Letters were written, and position papers were shared in the 1770s which advanced the cause of freedom in America, prior to the Revolution that began in 1775, and was codified on July 4, 1776. We need to do the same today. The internet can help greatly, but as recent events show, that communication option has been severely compromised by this government and the woke left. In fact, only concerned citizens can write letters, state positions, or point out criminal wrongs, and necessary changes. I will be doing this from now on, and I invite all Americans who are concerned with these issues to join me.

As I see matters, various militia groups on the right are already in place, as they were in the 1770s, and another one of these is not needed. It is my hope that our current military will, when the time comes, choose to uphold the US Constitution and not merely kowtow to the whims of our demented, crime encumbered president. We shall see on that score. I mean, after all members of the military swore an oath to uphold the US Constitution, not an oath to the president. We'll wait and see where the military stands when the time comes.

What is needed today is direction for a conservative, Christian based, save America movement, which takes place outside of the political context. Any political candidate will always be suspected of promoting himself or herself, rather than promoting the conservative agenda itself. We need to step outside of that political process into the realm of thought, as did Thomas Paine and Samuel Adams in the 1770s. These men didn't run for office, or hold office continually, nor did they seek personal power. They wrote for, and agitated for, freedom. We need serious men and women of all races, all faiths, coming together to discuss changing our political system within the bounds of the US Constitution, such that the governmental tyranny we see today at the federal level is much less possible. We need to stop the politically woke attacks on Christians and conservatives. We need to foster the idea that political disagreements can be managed by reasoned debate and elections, if both sides are honest. Of course, in today's world, the woke, leftist democrats aren't.

Message for democrats: My silence doesn't mean I agree with you. It's just that your level of stupidity and dishonesty has left me completely speechless.

It was for this reason that the original constitution set up the three branches of government. By dividing federal power, you tend to dilute it, and that preserves individual freedom. Also, our founding fathers limited federal power further with the reserved powers clause in the US Constitution (look that one up for a good lesson in what has gone wrong in America today). Specifically, the framers of our Constitution prohibited the federal government from doing anything not specifically designated as a federal power by the Constitution. Thus, there should be no department of education and no fbi. Both education and policing functions are powers reserved for the states by the Constitution. Given the corruption of the current department of injustice, the irs, and fbi, one can see clearly that if one man—in this case our demented president—controls the most powerful policing agency in the country, he can easily use that agency to discredit or even indict and/or jail his political opponents. That is exactly what is happening today! It has recently been shown that several former members of the federal department of injustice were employed by the New York district attorney Bragg's office, before that office in New York indicted President Trump—Biden's political opponent! This is banana republic politics, and is unprecedented in America until now, and Biden is doing it in my country! I can no longer stand by doing nothing.

The US Constitution specifically forbids the federal government from branching out into policing and these other areas; those powers are reserved for the states. We'll have to start our revised federal government by returning to the wisdom embodied in the US Constitution, and eliminating the fbi and the department of education. This is one move to make immediately. Now is the time for conservatives to speak up. Perhaps Thomas Paine said it best scores of years ago.

"These are the times that try men's souls. The summer soldier and the sunshine patriot will, in the crisis, shrink from the service of his country, but he that stands NOW deserves the thanks of man and woman."

So be it; on this sacred holiday, on this July 4, 2023, I will do more than merely eat a hotdog and watch fireworks. I will stand up. For me, that means I will think, I will write, and I will work to re-establish our great nation. I'll offer this diary, these thoughts, and others, and subsequently my full time labor services, to any conservative organization working to preserve freedom in this country, and I'll happily do that without pay.

One of my forefathers fought with General Washington in the American Revolution, and my father fought for this country in WW II. I want to preserve the country they fought for, and not the Biden crime family, or a leftist-envisioned, politically correct nightmare we have today. With that heritage in mind, I can do no less.

So here is the invitation for you. Join me, and we'll soon join others, and be joined by others. We are not revolutionaries—we merely want to revitalize the government assured to us by the US Constitution, and the freedom to express our Christian conservative opinions without being attacked or "canceled." We will be a strong voice toward movement in that direction. Most importantly we are, AND WILL BE free Americans. We will be political without seeking office ourselves. Specifically, we will operate by communication with other like-minded folk, by seeking candidates who stand up for Constitutional principles, and we will be heard. I've already written multiple times to my Congressman Andrew Clyde, another man whom I deeply respect. I URGE YOU TO WRITE YOURS! SEND THAT CONGRESSMAN A COPY OF THIS!

Moreover, this letter is a beginning. I invite you to write your own letter, start your own dialogue on your concerns, and then share them with your congressman and me.

Contact me if you wish. I will be doing everything I can to make a difference. Someone has to, and I can wait no longer.

Postscript: After I wrote the reflection above, Senator Grassley released one of the documents that the fbi had held back, in their obvious attempt to protect the Biden crime family.

Form FD- 1023 was released on 7/20/23. This fbi document details Biden influence peddling involving an investigation of corruption in a foreign country. Biden, as vice president used his influence in a foreign country, by threatening to withhold American Aid (our tax dollars) unless a prosecutor in that country was fired. After he was fired, Biden got paid for his illegal services via Hunter Biden's shell companies. This is clear bribery by a sitting Vice President, who is now our President. Based on this document, as of July 21, 2023, many more House members and senators are now calling for the impeachment of Joe Biden. You can't make this stuff up, folks.

Postscript Two: On August 13, a Republican Congressmember from Florida filed impeachment charges against Joe Biden, based on the ongoing revelations stemming from the republican investigations in Congress, and uncovering the bank records showing that the President, when he was Vice President, took bribes for certain actions, as described above. This begs the question, can one impeach a demented president?

REFLECTION 2:

Victimhood, Racism, and Black Democrats

(Initially written 7/15/23)

While my first reflection detailed many concerns and fears I have with our crime driven federal government, I want to step back from those concerns and discuss a broader reach of fears on the ongoing existence of the United States of America. I fear that our shared belief in America, what some have called American Exceptionalism, is dying at the alter of victimhood, best represented today by the woke left—critical race theory, and ongoing discussions of reparations for slavery. "Victimization" seems to be the badge of honor on the woke left, and the connecting principle between various groups.

Of course, You can pick your victim class out of the headlines any given day (Black Americans, Native Americans, women, Trans individuals, Muslims, etc.). Still, while anyone can choose to become a victim, others exposed to the same experiences and circumstances choose not to be a victim. Here is another harsh truth. America will not long survive increased, self-chosen "victimhood!"

We Americans, as a population, have always shared a belief in rational, honest self-government, and based on that, our nation has grown and thrived for over 250 years, while ever expanding the freedoms offered to various groups in this nation. If however that belief fails, or is abandoned

9

by most Americans as various groups claim victimhood, we will cease to be a country. To put it simply, "victims" of America will generally not support America, and this noble experiment in self-government will be lost.

As I pointed out previously, our nation will not long survive with a criminal family in the White House, particularly with all democrats blindly supporting that family. However, one major concern within that democratic support is the determination of most Black Americans to blindly support all democrats, including that Biden crime family. The two senators from Georgia, one black and one white, are both democrats, and neither has responded to me on the issue of the Biden laptop evidence against our criminal president and his son. I find these democrats to be unresponsive to me, one of their constituents, if not downright dishonest in this regard—they would rather support their party at all costs, than do what is right to assure the rule of law in our nation. Again, unless something changes quickly, our nation will not survive.

With that said, why then do particular groups, such as Black Americans support this rogue democratic party? It was, historically, the democrats that defended slavery, fostered Jim Crow laws, and fought against the famed Civil Rights Act and Voting Rights Act in previous decades. Why should Black Americans support that party?

Further, it behooves one to ask, what are the real results of slavery and Jim Crow laws, and are we still seeing the results of slavery or Jim Crow today in our American society? Does this background of oppression predispose Black Americans to support democrats somehow?

Today, Black Americans seem to believe that the democratic party supports them more so than do republicans. While there are notable exceptions (Senator Tim Scott, or Candice Owen), there is this lingering idea that to be Black, one must support democrats. Of course, this support was specifically fostered by democratic leaders over the years. After all, President Lyndon Johnson, the Southern democrat who largely created today's "welfare state" in America, commented on his "war on poverty programs" and was reported to have stated to two governors while riding on Air Force One:

"**I'll have those n*ggers voting democratic for the next 200 years!**"

(see **The Democratic Party's Two-Facedness of Race Relations | HuffPost Latest News**). Thus, one could argue, that Black Americans were targeted intentionally, with the welfare state handouts, and today this group may have a monetary interest in voting for democrats, despite the anti-black, overtly racist history of this party. This seems to be the only reason that makes sense.

Further, since the 1960s, democrats have repeatedly voted for ever increasing taxation and increased spending on various social programs. These are the very social programs that one Black Historian, Dr. Thomas Sowell, has suggested destroyed the Black American family. Thus, it is reasonable to conclude that these social support programs have, in fact, harmed the Black American community at least as much as these funds have helped. In this manner the democratic party has made Black Americans "victims" of America, and the money flows to the victimized. Further, money is money and if the democrats are more willing to provide unearned funds to certain classes or subgroups of people then those people will typically support them with their vote. Democrats seem to love nothing more than being perceived as the party that supports the downtrodden—the victims of any unfairness, whether real or imagined.

Ever listened to a democrat make a point, and wondered, "Who ties your shoes for you?"

It is interesting to note that some Black American leaders are calling for more honesty in discussions of which political party Black Americans should support. This would include such leaders as Candice Owen, historian Thomas Sowell, and Senator Tim Scott. Senator Scott, for example, is a republican conservative Christian, and his views and mine rarely diverge. He has seen through the dishonest hype that has characterized democratic *talking points for years, regarding political affiliation. He has been called a racist, and "Uncle Tom" and various other insulting names, in spite of his skin color. Still, Senator Scott is running for the republican nomination for president this year, and apparently is one of the top three republican candidates. I support his career, even though he is not my senator. It will be interesting to watch over time, this Christian Black American leader.*

We should note that calling Senator Scott racist does show the limited intellectual capabilities of the woke left. It also leads anyone with a brain to conclude the following tongue-in-cheek definition is true:

Racist --anyone who wins an argument with a liberal.

Of course, that term "racist" is flung around in almost every argument offered by the woke left, which in and of itself is a sign of flagging intellectual capability. In today's world everyone who is white is presumed to be racist, but this trend of infantile name calling is much more damaging than at first appears. In one instance, a white Principal in Canada, was publicly labeled as racist and "white supremacist" by an "diversity, equity, and inclusion" trainer employed by the school district. That training was, of course, based on several fundamental concepts from critical race theory—i.e. all cultures are systematically racist, and all white people are racist, and must "examine their whiteness!" When the principal disagreed with the premise that Canada was basically a racist nation, the equity trainer armed with righteousness indignation no doubt, started this childish name-calling. As a result, the principal, by all accounts a serious, well qualified educator who always had his student's interests at heart, fell into a rather serious emotional distress. He then filed a lawsuit against the school district, that forced him into such training. He may have been concerned with the damage that this name-calling would do when it inevitably passed through the faculty to his students, but we'll never know his intentions beyond what was stated in the lawsuit. Ultimately, his depression won out and he committed suicide.

With that death in mind, we need to consider the definition above in a new light. How much destruction is taking place in the name of "equity training" "DEI training" or CRT in Canada and the USA today? Further, once teachers are required to undergo these district enforced trainings, these harmful myths, or at best, half-truths, will then be used to call our public school students destructive names. Is that fair to our students? In the name of DEI, our sons and daughters are specifically taught today that they are systematically racist, in states which force this training on public school faculty! According to some recent news stories, today eating is considered racist; the Body Mass Index long used to help persons of all colors understand the issues of weight control is racist, and even camping in a state or national park is racist. Apparently, everything is racist, and this untruth is being forced-fed to our children. How much emotional distress should we and our white or Asian children be subject too?

I could discuss much more the question of real racism, vs. the faux-racism which has been "imagined" into existence by proponents of critical race theory and other intellectually limited leftist thinkers, but for now I'll just offer a couple of statements that are true. These are things that woke, liberal ideologues never seem to grasp.

If everything is racist, then nothing is racist. If you cry "wolf" at everything, sooner or later no one will pay any attention anymore.

No proposition, belief, or statement is racist, if it is true.

But these thoughts still leave us with the question of why any Black American would support democrats? Perhaps the question is simply unanswerable; this may represent one of the "quantum holograms" of politics; like the quantum hologram in physics, "It's there, it's real, but it doesn't make any sense!" For now, we'll just leave this question here.

We can note that the old Civil Rights leaders are dying off, and a newer generation of Black American leaders have begun to take their place, and some are beginning to question the undying support of democrats by Black Americans. Many of those leaders likewise challenge the falsehoods of critical race theory (e.g. Dr. Thomas Sowell, Senator Scott of South Carolina). One can only hope for more honesty and integrity from the left. Perhaps one day *they will become less racist themselves and may even be able to actually listen to these emerging Black American conservatives, and thereby learn something new.*

REFLECTION 3:

Where My Reparations?

(written initially on 7/15/23)

The reparations headlines from the news today are new, but over the last few years, this issue has been studied in various states such as California, Oregon, Georgia, and elsewhere. It has been suggested that white owned businesses should pay an extra tax in order to pay Black Americans for slavery, or past racial injustices, or for "stealing our bodies, our land, and our culture." As nearly as I can determine, the pro-reparations argument is based on the following main idea; white men stole blacks from Africa, taking them from their families, and cutting them off from their culture, while bringing them to America and making them slaves. The difficulties in Black America today are traced directly to this history of evil white men and this evil of slavery and subsequent discriminations destroyed the identify and culture of Black Americans. Therefore, white Americans should pay Black Americans for this oppression.

Historically, not much of this proposition is true. There is no historical evidence that any white American plantation owner ever entered Africa, stole people from their homes, and sold them into slavery in America. That simply didn't happen. Rather, blacks in various African tribes practiced slavery well before the Atlantic slave trade developed--as did almost all cultures in the world. Next, in the African slave trade from the 1600s through the early 1800s, Blacks most often sold other blacks to Muslim slave

15

traders. Sometimes those sold were captives in inter-tribal warfare in Africa, while others were merely undesirable members of the tribe. There were also numerous instances in which Muslim slave traders simply captured blacks and sold them into slavery. Also, some of the richest slave traders in Africa were Blacks (Tippu Tip, was one example), and thus, blacks by and large sold blacks mostly to Muslims, who then moved the newly acquired slaves to the African coast where the slaves were sold to ship captains for the middle crossing, a horrific trans-Atlantic journey in the cramped belly of a slave ship.

From the 1600s until the 1800s, those slave ship captains were most often British, Dutch, or Portuguese. However, by the 1800s, some ship captains were Americans, mostly from New England. Those "slavers" then transported their human cargo mainly to Brazil, the Caribbean sugar islands, or middle and south America. Only about 2% or 3% of all slave ships that ever left the African coast were bound directly for North America. As slavery grew in all thirteen colonies in British North America, the colonies that subsequently became states, the institution became much more frequent in the southern states. In those states, white plantation owners, black businessmen, and native Americans all owned slaves. In Georgia, for example, it is well documented that at least two Cherokee plantation owners each owned scores of slaves. Thus, while the vast majority of plantation owners were white, not all were.

While slavery was a cruel vicious historical reality all over the world, these historical realities show that there is no group or culture that is "innocent" of the horrors of slave trading. To suggest that slavery is a product of "evil white men in American" is simply not true. History shows that, when it comes to slavery, there is plenty of guilt to go around for all races and cultures, so perhaps everyone should pay reparations. For example, it is interesting to watch a historic presentation on the Top 10 Black Slave Owners **(Top 10 Black Slaveowners - YouTube).** ***Should descendants of those Black folks pay reparations too?***

However, the pro-reparations argument goes much further, to suggest that slavery so handicapped Black Americans that they cannot recover from this, and thus, that they have continued to be treated unfairly. The various Jim Crow laws, proposed and supported by democrats in the old South, provide clear evidence of such post-slavery discrimination. The pro-reparations argument also includes the stated assumption that even today, Black Americans are handicapped financially because of slavery and it's Jim Crow aftermath. Based on this incorrect thinking, most liberal Blacks argue for reparations for Black Americans and no one else.

What is any intelligent man to make of this selfish, historically inaccurate, one-sided claim for reparations? Moreover, on the whole, is the argument for reparations valid? Can society merely pay money to correct wrongs that ended over some 160 years ago? Should we even try to do so?

Only a few decades ago in 1988, President Reagan, a Republican, offered an apology to Americans of Japanese descent who were interred during WW II. Also $20,000 was paid in financial reparations to those living that year. Personally, I believe that was morally correct; paying reparations to living individuals who were discriminated against seems to be the right thing to do. However, there is a vast difference between paying living victims of discrimination, and trying to correct some wrong of 160 years ago. Paying for historical wrongs simply will not work for a number of reasons, but here's a thought!

Let's just agree to the idea of reparations! Let everyone in America who ever owned a slave, pay ten thousand dollars to everyone in America who ever was a slave! Problem Solved!

Here are a few more particulars. If we pay descendants of victims of historic wrongs, everyone on earth should get paid! On the face of the matter, one can argue that if our goal is to pay for historical injustices, then almost all individuals on the planet should receive reparations for some injustice or another! First of all, almost every population anywhere in the world, has at one time or another been displaced, forced to move out of their native land, or in some military action or another dispossessed of land and culture. The Irish Potato famine, as one example displaced many thousands of starving people, forcing them to move into a life of abject poverty and squalor in many American cities. Those Irish certainly faced overt prejudice in America, as did Italian Americans, Greeks, and virtually every other immigrant group. Are we to conclude that almost everyone is a victim of cultural displacement or discrimination in America? Does this mean reparations for everyone?

Some have suggested that any land or wealth acquired as a result of the oppression associated with displacing a people or culture during the colonial period of world history should be returned to rightful owners, a sort of "reparations by property" idea. Still, it is a simple, straightforward fact that almost all land on the planet has been conquered at one time or another by some army either recently or in antiquity, and such warfare historically results in massive displacements and other significant changes for members of indigenous societies. Should all land therefore be returned to rightful owners, or should the descendants of those owners be compensated somehow?

Should the entire continents of North and South America be "given back" to Native American tribes? Should Israel be given back to Arabs, or Persians, or Egyptians, or even Italians (after all, let's remember that the Italian empire, "Rome" ruled Israel 2000 years ago, and all of those peoples ruled Israel at one time or another!)? Perhaps South Africa should be given back to the remnants of various tribes who owned that land hundreds of years ago. With this history of the world in mind, the "return the land" idea does not seem to be really workable.

But financial reparations involve much more personal issues than merely what lands have been overtaken or destroyed by invading armies. Here the argument is, "our ancestors were oppressed, and some discrimination continues that has negatively impacted we Black Americans today, so we are due financial reparations."

Again, any honest person will quickly realize that Black Americans do not hold exclusive "rights" to having been oppressed. Personally, my white

German ancestor was sold into indentured servitude on the docks of the town of New Bern in the North Carolina colony around 1710. He had no parents, no money, and he was about 6 years old at the time. Now, such indentured servitude was not life-long in most cases, while the slavery of American Indians (who were really the first slaves captured and sold as slaves by Europeans in America) or Blacks (captured in Africa) generally was lifelong as well as generational in nature. Slavery was clearly a much more cruel living situation than indentured servitude in most cases. Still, indentured servitude was oppression, and it was certainly not a giant bell ringer for climbing the social ladder! Thus, descendants of indentured servants represent a victim class! I and my own family were victimized! So let's ask the question: where are my reparations? Shouldn't I get paid, perhaps for historic oppression? Indentured servitude was victimization—unpaid labor for simple room and board.

I'm a victim! Where's my money?

What about Native Americans? After all, Europeans stole this entire continent from them, the Indian wars lasted nearly three hundred years--from 1587 until well into the 1880s, whereas slavery ended in American in 1865. Thus, victimization of Native Americans is more recent than victimization of Black slaves. Aren't Native Americans still victimized today? Thus, are not these tribal peoples due for higher reparations than Black Americans based on that fact? Further, shouldn't all the land stolen from them be returned?

Within the last week, an ice cream maker in America (a wealthy, white, male ice cream maker, of all people) has made such a suggestion of returning "stolen" land to Native Americans, and he was widely ridiculed for it. It was then pointed out that the very land his corporate headquarters sits on was once, Indian land, and a local tribal leader offered to discuss with him the repatriation of that land! Should he give that back?

All of this begs the fundamental question, can we attribute today's societal ills—financial disparities between the races, or the breakdown of the Black American family—to slavery and Jim Crow laws, or perhaps to ongoing presumptive "systematic racism" in America? And if so, should our nation pay reparations for these evils?

The Historian Thomas Sowell, a Black man himself, has noted that today's failure of Black families has little to do with slavery or Jim Crow, regardless of the poor weak arguments for "reparations" found in the headlines today. Rather, Dr. Sowell points out that as late as the 1960s most Black Americans lived in two parent families and supported themselves. Neither slavery nor it's bastard child, Jim Crow, but rather the War on Poverty and other federal programs of the 1960s and 1970, destroyed the Black American Family, and Dr. Sowell provided the evidence for that assertion, in terms of the number of intact Black American families over time. He concluded that those governmental programs alienated fathers and provided more funds for producing more children outside of the traditional family. Thus, many Black American kids, both then and now, were raised without the influence of a loving father.

While some children do alright in life without having had such an early paternal influence, many do not. A loving father in the family, rather than the mother (who loves children unconditionally), represents societal perspectives in the family, and fosters the development the self-discipline and reflective self-control required to live successfully in any civilized society. Without that loving paternal influence, one tends to get kids raised with little self-discipline and these kids often fail as adults in society. This breeds the development of a "victim class" who believe they have always been victims, and are thus "owed" societal support, either through government programs or through such things as reparations. Victimhood members of this type see victimization everywhere, and will ultimately abandon their general support of society overall. This results in the headlines we see today, some 60 years after President Johnson created the welfare state, with his War on Poverty.

These programs, taken together, have destroyed the Black American family, as well as any sense among some Black Americans that they can *develop opportunities for themselves, by using the free education provided in the USA, while strengthening their families, and developing a serious work ethic. Black children today are taught to be victims of the presumptive "systemic racism" in America, a systemic racism that some Black American leaders like Senator Tim Scott of South Carolina say does not exist. Still, Black children today are taught to be victims and not successful learners, workers, voters, or participants in democracy. These children are taught that systematic racism and/or "white privilege" oppresses them. Now, in an earlier social media post, I once proposed a definition of White Privilege.*

White Privilege = Success resulting from good parenting + education + a strong work ethic.

With that in mind, the argument for reparations becomes meaningless. In fact, one could argue that reparations have been paid already, via our safety net societal programs, generally inexpensive or free health care for lower economic class individuals, and the provision of a free education to all. These are our reparations. Thus, the reparations debt has been paid, every single day, for many years now!

But here is the real rub. Black Americans have largely bought into the belief that they are victims of "white oppression" in America, rather than participants in America. They often ignore historical facts such as the fact that the first American killed in the American Revolution was a Black American, or that the first person to legally own slaves in America was a Black man. They ignore the fact that many free Blacks owned slaves in America, as did many Native Americans. They ignore the fact that slavery was practiced in Africa, and world-wide--well before the Atlantic slave trade existed. Should we attempt to obtain reparations from various countries in Africa? How's that going to work out?

Ignoring history will not change facts, and pretending that white Americans are the only oppressors in all of history is simply ignorance. Still, this twisted perception of reality creates and justifies victimhood, and such victimhood could well be the demise of America. If persons do not buy into the noble experiment of self-government, but rather, choose to be victims, then any responsibility to meaningfully contribute to self-government flies out the window. Victims will ignore facts, reality, and history, in order to argue for their own narrow interests, and again that leads to things like Antifa, Black Lives Matter, the idolization of a petty criminal like George Floyd, and selfish, one- sided arguments for reparations. With each generation becoming more aggressive in their self-chosen victim status, each generation will argue for more, more, more, all to come from the pockets of the evil white men in society. This argument is obvious today, in the many committees (several in California, one or two in Georgia, and elsewhere) set up to study reparation exclusively for Black Americans.

I despair when I see these discussions in our society. I believe that America depends on members of our society buying into and believing in what many have called American Exceptionalism. Without a sense of loyalty to that ideal—an ideal rarely taught in schools today—our society will not long survive. Just this past week, my wife and I were discussing the dishonesty of many leaders of BLM—those Black Lives Matter leaders who used much of the 90 million raised in 2020 that flooded into their accounts, not for betterment of lives of Black Americans, but to buy personal mansions, and enrich only themselves. At some point in that discussion it dawned on me that many Black Americans no longer believe in America at all. If anything, America for them is not the nation that granted them education, opportunity, and freedom, but rather an oppressor nation, which they must fight against. I told my wife at that moment that our nation cannot survive this.

Here are a few related points. Does anyone really believe that America could put an army into the field today, that would be the equal the Greatest Generation of the 1940s? Would our nation fight an evil, as personified in another Hitler today, given that so many have seemingly opted out of the American dream? Maybe our Hitler in today's terms is Putin (who is grabbing up more and more of Eastern Europe) or North Korea, a new nuclear power, or Iran, or China. Who knows? Can our nation stand against these enemies, if called upon to do so?

I fear not. With a weak, demented President in the White House, supported blindly by democrats, and a large and growing victim class who do not believe in our American Experiment, would we find the will to fight for freedom, should another Hitler arise? Would American even begin to defend itself, when it is as divided as it is today?

Again, I despair when I see serious men and women argue for reparations for only one group, when almost every American could make a viable argument for the same thing. Further, such payments would be untenable, if not outright impossible. Finally, participation in the American experiment is, in and of itself, reparations for all. In fact, all have the opportunity to make of themselves what they will; just look at the successes of General Colin Powell, Dr. Condoleezza Rice, Dr. Thomas Sowell, Rev. Jesse Jackson, Mayor Andrew Young, Dr. Martin Luther King, Senator Tim Scott, and thousands upon thousands of other Black Leaders. Leaders like these belie the fictious arguments for reparations and tend to prove the equation on white privilege noted above.

Still, with so many persons choosing to participate in victimhood rather than building for themselves the life of an American Dream, our nation may not survive. The image of American Exceptionalism, and belief in that concept make it a reality for many, who then create for themselves a wonderful life. As more persons of whatever complexion abandon that dream, we will lose ourselves and ultimately our country.

Postscript: Mr. Larry Elder, a Black Leader and Candidate for President in 2024, appeared on the Fox News Business on August 13, proclaiming the same thing noted above; that the problem of ever increasing crime in America, largely involves the Black American subculture, and specifically the problem of fatherlessness in the Black community. This is the same point as that made by History Prof. Thomas Sowell, discussed above. The lack of discipline and self-control among many young Blacks stem from the fact that 70% of young Black kids today are raised in homes without a father. Mr. Elder pointed to the high levels of crime to be committed by Black People, most of which is directed at other Black people, and then he correctly points to fatherlessness as the ultimate culprit. Thank God for Black Leaders of courage who will state the truth!

REFLECTION 4:

The Problem of Whiteness

(written initially on 7/17/23)

Today mainstream media, throughout much of the world has bought into a big lie, a false narrative propagated by proponents of critical race theory that being white is equivalent with being guilty of racism, that all Blacks are victims of oppression, and that white privilege and systemic racism in America actually exist today. All of this has the consistency, the texture, the color, and the smell of horse feces (figure this one out for yourself, I'll wait!).

Today's example of such excretions is represented by the course title above, "The Problem of Whiteness." This is a real course title at the University of Chicago. This course title is intentionally, highly offensive, as it seems to codify a set of unproven assumptions, and likewise seems to represent overt prejudices against all white people. These are core principles of critical race theory, but more importantly, this is the very type of racism that Dr. Martin Luther King fought against all his life.

Now if someone dared to title a course "The Problem of Blackness" one might only imagine the name calling and pure hatred that professor would endure for such a course title. Still, here is the course: "The Problem of Whiteness." The set of assumptions inherent in such a title, along with most of critical race theory is, simply put, absurd.

Apparently the offensive title is perfectly OK with the University of Chicago (see a discussion of this on You Tube: **College slammed for its 'Problem with Whiteness' course - YouTube)***. This course along with most of critical race theory remains a theory--an unproven construct--that has unfortunately become the swan song of many liberal woke thinkers. In the Chicago case, one courageous white student noticed the obvious racism and highlighted this course title in a twitter post, correctly labeling it racist. This student has now been called every name one might imagine (racist, instigator of violence, etc.), and has been removed from various campus groups as "too extreme," simply because he told the truth. Apparently, according to the woke leftist who promote critical race theory, simply disagreeing with any of their premises is enough to prove that someone is, in fact, racist. The Professor of that course even fought to get the student expelled from the University. In fact, he has now suffered so much for that honest political opinion, that he is taking his story to the press. I saw the student speak on a short segment on Stewart Varney (Fox News) this morning. Varney pointed out that the professor of that course stated that whiteness is "damaging." I'm not clear on exactly what that means nor was Varney, but it would not seem to make any white person feel comfortable, and may make many students feel very uncomfortable. Again, this seems to be one of the goals of critical race theory—condemn all white people via pre-judgement, without considering the facts, and decry (i.e. cancel) them for being racist once they disagree.*

The student has invited other white students who experienced such anti-white racist hatred similar to this to speak up. He argued that Universities should be places of free expression, exchange of ideas, and valuing many viewpoints rather than bastions for such racist, anti-white hatred such as that represented in this course title. He's right. He should not be made to feel like a second- class citizen because of the color of his skin. No one, of any race should.

Well, there is just so much to be said on this one. First of all, compliments to that student for his honesty and courage. He'll suffer much more from the woke ideologues on the left as they continue their campaign of cancellation against him, no doubt, but it is way past time for all persons to demand an end to all racism, and that includes anti-white racism. I admire this student's courage.

Next, we have to note that this is not an isolated event. For example, similar courses have been offered at an Arizona school, among others. Further, critical race theory has invaded our public schools as well as our colleges. A new book, "School of Woke, How Critical Race Theory Infiltrated American Schools and Why We Must Reclaim Them," by Kenny Xu documents the failure of many liberal school districts in helping Black students move forward, when compared with many districts in more conservative areas like Mississippi and Louisiana. Xu ties critical race theory, which is specifically taught to children in democratic run cities like Baltimore, Chicago, and New York, to victimology. Thus the horrid, unproven, and uncriticized ideas of critical race theory essentially become a self-fulfilling prophecy, which has infected public schools in many areas, as well as colleges and universities. In fact, Xu states the issue, using fact based arguments, rather bluntly; "I'm exploring why these policies that are instituted in the name of diversity, equity and inclusion and critical race theory are in fact harming children" (as quoted on FoxNew on July 31, 2023).

In a similar vein, Vivek Ramaswamy, argued that these woke ideologies had likewise infested many American businesses. In his book Woke, Inc. Inside Corporate America's Social Justice Scam, this successful businessman documented how American businesses, advertising, etc. had bought into this woke ideology, while unblinkingly moving into ever increasing wokeness. Of course, this is exactly what led to the recent downfall of "Bud Light!"

Inherent in this wokeness is the basic belief that all whites are racist, and that there is systematic, anti-black bias that permeates our society. Here is the title of an article by Brandes Gress, which I found in my online news feed (on 8/9/23). It is from the medical field and demonstrates this axiom, of "systematic racism of all whites."

"Are all Nurses Racist? Kentucky Nurses to Complete "Structural Racism" and "White-Spaining" courses to Address "Implicitly Bias" or Risk Disciplinary Action."

A few days later on 8/16/23 I found a similar headline: Doctors file a lawsuit against California over mandatory training claiming "White individuals are naturally racist."

As these articles imply, medical professionals are often required to participate in the false "wokeism" fostered by critical race theory, and in some cases, they will suffer dire consequences. So here we are. College courses, the medical field, and almost all of corporate America is now not only exposed to this "all whites are racist" propaganda, but are implementing required courses, and forcing this false axiom of critical race theory down the throats of millions of Americans.

With the Bud Light beer use of a "trans" woman in advertising, and the clear backlash from that (reports indicated that literally scores of millions of dollars were lost by that add), we have to note that Americans are, increasingly waking up to the stupidities of the woke left.

Still, critical race theory, and the inherent dishonesties and half-truths therein, permeate most businesses, industries, and educational institutions today. Further how many people have been forced to sit through "diversity, equity, and inclusion" training on the job, while biting their lip to keep their mouth shut as they were, directly or indirectly, labeled racist or white supremacist during that training? The news is filled with stories in which some leftist oriented racist invites, or requires white persons to "examine their whiteness" or we read of some leftist individual making the ridiculous argument that persons (i.e. Black Americans) who are not in power cannot be racists. This is all part and parcel of critical race theory, a truly stupid set ideas overall, that some liberals are taking way to seriously.

I will note that if you want to see racism at its worst, watch the events unfold when a white male wanders into a predominately Black bar some Saturday evening. You cannot have such an experience and still argue that

Blacks cannot be racists. The hard fact is, every human being can be racist; all can prejudge others based on skin color, religious preference, tattoos one might have, eating habits, how one dresses, or virtually anything else.

With that stated, the best example we have for appropriate human behavior is Jesus—a man who looked at the character of a person rather than their skin color, political beliefs, occupation, or religion. One may only hope that one day, we all live in a world peopled by persons seeking to become more like Jesus in that regard.

Still, what are we to make of this course title, and this call to "examine one's whiteness?" If by that these ideologues mean that all of us, persons of every race and religion, should examine ourselves for prejudices, and to the degree possible rid ourselves of them, I'd agree. In fact, I'd consider that perspective quite biblical. Jesus was not above hanging out with prostitutes, sinners and tax collectors—the very persons that Jewish culture and prejudices of the day demanded he avoid. Further, what is the story of the Good Samaritan about if not a person of one racial group assisting, without prejudice, a person of another race?

However, that's not what proponents of critical race theory mean. Again, the title of this course says it all: The Problem of Whiteness.

It is an axiom of the left that only white people hold power, and thus only white people can be racist. These persons ignore all the situations in which Black Americans hold power, apparently pretending that such situations do not exist. Of course, the proposition itself is laughable on the face of it. Are we to believe that racism doesn't exist in areas of the world where there are no Caucasians? Are not various "high born" people in India, as one example prejudiced against certain persons of a lower class? Is the caste system not a reality in India? Do these leftist thinkers really believe their own assertion that one must be white to be a racist, or hold political power to be racist? If so, they are either stupid or ill informed. If they choose to ignore these realities, they are being completely dishonest, and will probably never be convinced of their own prejudice against white people. Thus, we probably should not spend much time trying to convince those folks of their errors. Their beliefs will ultimately go the way of the "flat earth" thinkers, and for the same reason; their fundamental beliefs are simply not true.

The Problem of Whiteness

Still, let's do what they request. Let's examine the "Problem of Whiteness," historically. First, in the USA both Black Americans and white Americans owned slaves. So did many Native Americans. Slavery existed in Africa before any European visited that continent, as it existed virtually everywhere, worldwide. However, in spite of that history, a group of white men in North America, (exclusively white men, to be exact) created a country based on a beautiful truth; "all men are created equal." While that commitment did not include either Black Americans or women in 1776, when it was codified into our National Identity, it certainly does today. This represents an expansion of freedom over time, which took place because of that singular belief, and largely at the hands of white men. America was also among the first nations in history to outlaw the Atlantic slave trade.

Next, as a result of mostly white legislators in every state, education has been provided for all in our nation, regardless of race. The state of North Carolina, for example, paid exactly the same for my personal education (Grades 1 – 12) as it did for every Black American child in the state. Next, approximately 250,000 white men died in the Civil War fighting for the Union, and one result of that struggle was freedom of all slaves in the land. To lock that freedom into place, a white male Congress passed the 13th Amendment to the US Constitution. That Amendment was originally devised and promoted by a white man (President Lincoln, a Republican) and passed by a congress made up almost exclusively of white men. More recently it was a predominately white, male US Congress that passed the voting Rights Act and the Civil Rights Act in the 1960s, mainly because of Republican members of Congress. Many democrats voted against those acts. Is this the "whiteness" these critical race theory ideologues mean? Is this the whiteness we are to examine?

Of course, we should note the fact that, as a result of these actions by white men, many Black Americans have joined the political process, and have become successful leaders in our nation, with more arising all the time. Personally, I support Senator Tim Scott, a Black American from South Carolina, and I look forward to his ongoing participation in America's leadership.

To summarize, the "Problem of Whiteness" then: (1) white males articulated the very core, scared ideal of freedom, that all men are created equal, and have striven ever sense to expand that freedom to all persons, all races, and all sexes; (2) hundreds of thousands of white males and scores of thousands of black males, via a costly and bloody war, freed the Black Race in America in the 1860s; (3) this country educates all children as equals, and when students choose to do so, they benefit greatly from that; (4) both whites and black, both men and women, demanded freedom for all to participate in our Democracy from the 1920s through today, and particularly in the 1960s; (5) specific legislation was passed to enforce one's right to vote, regardless of skin color; (6) our nation today fosters Black American leaders across the political spectrum. Is this the problem of Whiteness to which critical race theory refers? Is this the examination of whiteness they seem to desire? Well, there is my examination of whiteness!

The Problem of Blackness

Now just for fun, here's a turn of thought. As a conservative Christian, I'd like to respectfully invite all Americans to honestly examine "The Problem of Blackness." If one's goal is to foster full, free, and equal participation by Black Americans in American society, integrity demands that we note a few things that might not be working out well in Black culture today.

We've already discussed the issue of fatherlessness in Black America, as have a number of Black intellectuals such as Dr. Sowell, Senator Tim Scott, and Mr. Larry Elder. With 70% of Black kids growing up without a father in the home, Black culture falls to the lowest common denominator of behavior; no father often equals no self-discipline. That is where we are today, as these leading Black intellectuals have stated.

We might next note, that in Black American culture today a wide variety of gang members, criminals, and drug dealers are held up to be honored, promoted as idolized heroes. This is the lowest common denominator for cultural leadership, and we have to ask, does this foster success in Black American culture? These venerated role models would include, for example Snoop-Dawg, a man whose only apparent talents are hip-hop music and smoking pot, but who nevertheless is all over the TV in various product endorsement adds. This particular "victim" of systematic racism makes millions by the way. America has been pretty sweet to him! We might also point to George Floyd, a drug dealer with more arrests on his record than Hunter Biden! His only apparent "talents" were a recurring ability to peddle drugs mostly to other blacks and to get arrested frequently, and in the final such instance, to get killed by an overzealous cop. Are these the role models one might wish to hold up to young Black American males? Since the death of Floyd, parks have been named after him and statues have arisen with his image. He is the poster boy of black lives matter! Still, is this the black role model of today? Is this who Black Americans want their male children to emulate?

But let our examination of Black Culture continue. Next, we might note that the hip-hop music that has arisen from many Black American artists is highly, offensive, very sexist, filled with hate, and extremely racist. The words used in that music (such as the N word, the F Word, bitches, hos, and numerous others) are the extremely hateful words that are banned in newspapers today. Also, if one listens to hip-hop, one can only assume that every woman on the planet—black or white, Asian, Inuit, or any other variety of female —is a "Ho," and a "Bitch." Some hip-hop songs seem to glorify rape, hatred, and anti-white prejudice, all of which is excused by the left as merely, some sort of semi-justified cultural anger of Black Americans. Still, do we really want our young persons listening to that crap? Is that what we want our daughters to hear? How might the ongoing popularity of such music impact our kids?

Another headline more recently involved thousands of blacks in South Africa shouting "Kill the Boer!" repeatedly (see various news stories on 8/7/23). The Boer people were white farmers, mainly of Dutch descent, living in South Africa and as a group, they have lived in that country for well over 300 years, but because they are white, they apparently deserve death. Of course, the woke media in America quickly justified that racist hatred as "not to be taken literally," but rather just an expression of rage by the Black population of that country. Still, a thinking man must ask, is this not overt anti-white hatred? Who can seriously believe that at least a few of those thousands of Blacks did not actually mean, "Kill the Boer?"

While my own child is now well into his 30s, I would not want he, or my granddaughters overly exposed to the obvious anti-white racism expressed in "kill the Boer," in hip-hop music, or in most of modern Black culture, including Critical Race Theory. I don't want them exposed to the horrid language, the cruses, the anti-white prejudices and pure hatred demonstrated in those ideologies, any more than I'd want them overly exposed to proponents of Nazism. In fact, I'd urge all parents to help their children avoid exposure to the harsh, racist and sexist language of hip-hop, as well as the half-truths and untruths of critical race theory.

If this position on my part looks like "systemic racism" to those racist, leftist ideologues who promote such theory, then so be it. Let me say it plainly; I don't like these aspects of Black American culture, and I don't believe they are a good influence on either white or Black Americans! Harsh language, prejudice, and hatred of any racial group was completely alien to the teachings of Jesus. Thus, I think these things do significant damage to young Black children, as well as white children and personally I don't want my family around these influences. If leftist liberals want their children exposed to hip-hop music, where all women are "hos" or "bitches" and Black Americans are "n*ggas," then that is their concern. I wish them the best in raising their children while promoting such horrible influences. Children raised within such hatred will begin to hate--that is a fact.

Still, the worst part of the Black subculture in America today is the sense of "victimhood" that is so emphasized for young children. This is another idea that is foundational to critical race theory—that all blacks are victims. Victims clearly, are not responsible for their own situation or circumstances. It is, from this vantage point, the "mean white man" and his "systemic racism" who is at fault if a Black cannot find a job, keep a job, or earn a decent living. Such failures are not viewed as a result of a personal choice to quit school, or fail to learn from the years one spent there. The concept of "Victimhood" tends to remove one from any personal responsibility, and to put it bluntly, anyone who chooses to define themselves as a victim, will soon become one. I want to say that again, because it is important.

Anyone who chooses to define themselves as a victim, will soon become one.

Thus, because critical race theory promotes this sense of victimhood, it is, in reality, doing a great disservice to all Black Americans. If you want Black Americans to fail in life, then support critical race theory! Here's another rub of victimhood. Once one chooses to be a victim—and it is always a choice—one tends to stay a victim. Victimhood always requires a new "evil one" whom the victim can blame, and such evil ones can always be found, after all, they are all white. Thus, victims will tend to stay victims. That is one reason that no amount of financial "reparations" which might be paid to a Black American is likely to drastically change that person's circumstances. Once one chooses to become a victim, that person tends to remain so.

Over the last couple of decades there has been clear evidence of this--that massive amounts of money will not significantly improve lives. We find this among the Cherokee Nation in North Carolina. After opening a casino on the reservation several decades ago, millions of dollars flowed into the Eastern Band of the Cherokee. The leaders decided to award $180,000 to each member of the tribe when they reached adulthood at the ripe old age of 18. Those funds could have been used for anything by the various tribal members—buying a nice home, or financing a powerhouse of a college education. However, the project was a miserable failure. After only a few years, the tribe had to revise that strategy and dole out those funds over an extended period of time to tribal members. What they found is that, when such a bonanza fell into the lap of an 18 year old, that kid tended to quit school, buy the fastest car they could find, and finance a totally irresponsible lifestyle until the money ran out. In short, few lives were changed for the better by receiving massive amounts of cash. Again, the "victims" remained victims, and the twin problems of the typical Native American reservation— suicide and drug addiction—are as high today among the Cherokee as they were four decades ago.

So here we are. According to critical race theory, white is evil, and all oppression results from evil white people, regardless of the freedoms we all now enjoy in America, freedoms that were created and defended by mainly white males. These historical facts, of course, should be ignored, because they do not conform to the narrative of critical race theory and Black victimhood. Further, any cultural expression, no matter how vile, racist, or sexist that is created by Black American figures is thus taken to represent "Black culture" and is deemed acceptable. On this basis, some leftist thinkers can actually try and justify something called "The Problem of Whiteness." Using this logic, some might even propose and begin to believe that "kill the Boer" is not a hateful, racist statement!

However, once again, integrity demands that we reject this perspective— the critical race theory subsumed in the course title, "The Problem of Whiteness." If anything, there is an ongoing "problem of blackness" as noted above, which is fostering Black American victims.

For this reason, those who care about an honest appraisal of history, not to mention the continuation of the American experiment and ongoing freedom, had better speak up soon, or, as the student above noted, this false set of leftists beliefs embodied in critical race theory will only become further codified into more college courses, or professional development workshops in various industries, and also, ultimately, into state and national law. Thus, the very real racism against whites, Asians, Mexican-Americans,

Native Americans and all others will only get worse. Further, I'd urge any supporters of the University of Chicago, or the other colleges fostering critical race theory to simply pull their funding.

More importantly, I'd like to eventually live in a world where racism in all its forms—racism against Blacks, against Jews, against Arabs, against whites, against Asians, against anyone else on the planet--has gone the way of cannibalism, hunter-gatherer cultures, pagan sun worship, or Nazism. Those ideologies and practices are largely dead today, and I hope to see a day when affirmative action, BLM, anti-white prejudice, and critical race theory are dead too! Most of these earlier ideas are supported or practiced today by much less than .01 % of those on the planet, but they will always be a part of history; let's leave them there! Of course, the same idea has been expressed much more honorably, and more beautifully by others.

"I look to a day when people will not be judged by the color of their skin, but by the content of their character." (Dr. Martin Luther King, from his "I Have A Dream" speech).

Or an even stronger, more beautiful statement.

"Do unto others, as you would have them do unto you" (Jesus: Luke 6:31).

REFLECTION 5:

Affirmative Action In My Lifetime

(written initially on 7/19/23)

Within the last month, the Supreme Court finally struck down Affirmative Action in college admissions in a case involving Harvard University and my own alma mater, the University of North Carolina. For anyone believing in freedom and fairness, this is wonderful news, but unfortunately, it comes 30 years too late. The inherent anti-white racism embodied in affirmative action programs was not only codified into law, it was practiced routinely throughout our nation for some 40 years, and it personally impacted me numerous times, as it does every successful Asian American and white American, even liberal whites!

I'm a white male who spent my working life in education, both public school and higher education. I can personally attest to the fact that Affirmative Action resulted in a very concrete racism against white males and Asians, at least in the field of education. Personally, I experienced this directly many times over a 32 year period from 1976 through 2008, as a job applicant and ultimately teacher and professor in the field of Education. Affirmative Action practices meant that when applying for jobs in education, I had to be a better, much more qualified job applicant than either women or Black Americans, in order to get the job. Moreover, I was twice denied a job because I was a white male, during the height of the "Affirmative Action" years, and in each case, my prospective employers confirmed that affirmative *action was the reason for that! While my personal case is only one example, many others have noted the same, so in this case, a couple personal examples might help illustrate the point. Here are the specifics.*

One Friday afternoon in 1976, I was interviewed and hired as a history teacher by a principal of a new high school, then being built in Jacksonville, NC. He told me to be in his office on Monday morning to sign a contract and complete paperwork for the job, so on Monday morning, I showed up. When I arrived at his office at 8:30, he looked at me with fear in his eyes, and said, "I tried to call you and save you the trip," (I'd had a 45 minute drive that morning, and this was pre-cell phones). He continued to inform me that "over the weekend" his school district had been informed by what was then the federal Department of Health, Education, and Welfare (HEW), that all of their "new hires" had to be Black teachers. Of course, the school district knew which teachers they were going to move into the new school, and that left only about 6 or 8 positions left to fill, and HEW, under Secretary Joe Califano had contacted the school district and let them know that they had to hire only Blacks for those teaching positions. Thus, did my government discriminate against me solely because I was a white male. It really pissed me off, but I shook the dust off my feet, as it were, and applied to graduate school instead.

Approximately a decade later, after completing a masters, several years teaching, and a doctorate, I applied for a position at Rutgers University. It was a 3 year tenure track position, with a research emphasis, and I was excited by that. I interviewed, along with two women, and I was considered the best candidate (so I was informed by the Department Chairperson), and I was offered the position! Great, except that when I got the contract to sign via mail, a week later it was not the 3 year, tenure track position I was applying for. I called the department chairperson and he explained to me that while I was the departmental faculty choice because of my several research publications, the University "equal rights" office had acted against my application. That office told the department chairperson that because the selection made by the faculty was a white male (me), and because there had been no Blacks in the applicant pool, the university could only offer me a one year, non-tenure track position. Further, if I wanted to keep the job, I would be required to reapply again the next year. I turned that job down, deciding to remain where I was. Thus, for the second time in my career, I was denied a position because I was white, even though I was the best candidate for that position according to the faculty making the selection. This was clearly overt discrimination.

However, about a week later, the same department chairperson called me to offer me, once again, the 3 year, tenure track position I had originally applied for. As it turns out, that department chair had "fought" for the right to hire me, because I was according to him the best applicant. He was willing to argue with the woke office on that campus for the best application, even if that applicant was white! I ultimately took that job. Still, here was clear evidence that my government, via the "equal rights" office at the university was discriminating against me.

Finally, I should note that in every application in education I've ever completed, on the bottom of the application, were those hateful, discriminatory words, "women and minority candidates encouraged to apply!" Thus, have I faced anti-white, anti-male prejudice in every job application I've ever done in my 32 years in education. Further, as a university faculty member for many years, I can't tell you how many times I was forced to sit on committees to try to "encourage" Black faculty to apply for a job, or times when I was told to "help out" a Black faculty member to get published, simply because of affirmative action. In my experience over 30 years, in the field of education, anti-white prejudice is alive and well.

In my weaker moments I've asked myself, is it necessary that white males pay this price of anti-white, anti-male discrimination? I've often thought that perhaps, it was necessary to pay this price of affirmative action, to help Blacks and women "catch up" somehow. Now, after being cancelled, and well past the end of my career, I have to ask, should my son, another white male, have to pay this price too, throughout the next 30 or 40 years, in his career? How about his white daughters? Is this a debt—this anti white discrimination—that has to be paid forever?

Now that's merely a bit of my story, but it is like many stories, in education, and presumably other fields. Since the 1970s, white candidates had to be better than any black candidates, or the black candidates would get the job. This is affirmative action; this is pure racism, and thank God the Supreme Court stopped it.

Still, there is much more to this story, involving how affirmative action hurt Black Americans. For this I turn to a recent report on Affirmative Action from the Heritage Foundation (How Affirmative Action at Colleges Hurts Minority Students Heritage Foundation: by E. Slatterly, 2015). That report details how affirmative action actually injures many, if not most Black Americans. Specifically, affirmative action takes some of the best and brightest Black Americans, and puts them in situations in which they will not succeed. As that report argues, the star of a high school basketball team is not likely to succeed if that person is moved directly into the NBA. Such a move would set them up to fail. Likewise placing moderately skilled Black scholars in schools which would otherwise be beyond their abilities sets them up to fail. One research study of students in a top law school found that more than 50% of those Black students, many of whom were affirmative action admissions, were in the bottom 10% of the class, and were twice a likely to drop out, as their white counterparts.

It's fairly easy to understand. Imagine an excellent Black Student who absent affirmative action, may have attended an excellent college such as University of North Carolina at Wilmington. However, other top universities were head hunting that student to meet an unstated racial quota because of Affirmative Action, so he might find himself or herself in the University of North Carolina at Chapel Hill, or perhaps Harvard or Princeton. Now all of these schools are good schools, but the Black Student in question, had he attended UNC Wilmington, would quite probably have excelled. However, if that same student goes to Princeton, he would probably find himself in the lowest 5 or 10 percent of the freshman class academically (Had I gone to Princeton, I would probably have found myself in the same position, but I would not have been admitted, being white). In such a case, the Black student may well have dropped out, or flunked out, of college.

The Heritage report called this impact of affirmative action an "academic mismatch" between the excellent student who would have succeeded admirably at UNC Wilmington, but failed out of Harvard, or Princeton, or UNC. This is truly tragic. It is unfair for the Black student to have been denied a successful college program, in order for some University to meet it's quota (most often unstated) of a certain percentage of Black students, and this practice denies our society another successful Black graduate of business school, or law school, or medical school. The data reported also show that once a highly successful Black student does flunk out or drop out of a top college where he or she was "mismatched," they are much less likely to reapply elsewhere. Thus, does Affirmative Action limit educational success for the best and brightest Black Americans. This reality, of course, hurts all Black Americans.

The report concludes that all students should be encouraged to enter schools in which their credentials are more evenly matched with their peers. In such schools, they are much more likely to succeed and ultimately graduate. In short, absent "affirmative action" Black students and all of society is much more likely to see more Black graduates, not fewer.

That report says it best;

"The harms of affirmative action are clear. Academic mismatch perpetuates low grades and high dropout rates for minority students who need a racial preference to gain admission. Basing admissions on race rather than merit also contributes to the dearth of minorities in STEM fields. No person should be disadvantaged by the color of his or her skin, no matter how sincere the intentions of affirmative action proponents," (Slatterly, 2015).

Every American should thank God that this racist abomination of affirmative action has now been terminated. Of course, affirmative action worked against me and many other white men and women, but it worked against the best and brightest black students too. The end to this racist practice has been too long in coming, and now our society will be better off. However, I now find reports of proponents of affirmative action at various *universities (Harvard is one example) seeking to undermine, or "get around" this ruling ending affirmative action, attempting to accomplish the same racist goals in other ways. Again, I hope to see an end to racism, including the well-intentioned racism of affirmative action. We'll just have to wait, and see, and be vigilant. It is a fact, that the woke left never sleeps.*

I talked to a woke democrat the other day who said our economy was just fine, thanks to Biden. Some of them still believe that crap. I just told him that he had made an ID ten T error. When he asked what that was, I told them to just write it down, and look at it. I hope he eventually got it!

ID   10   T   IDIOT

REFLECTION 6:

Term Limits and The Politics of The Fall

(Initially written 7/31/23)

How old is too old to govern? This is becoming a serious question in today's world, as our leaders across the political spectrum advance in years. Our country seems predisposed to elect or re-elect leaders who are not cognitively competent, who consistently fall down, and who cannot clearly express themselves. This raises a number of issues. Should all candidates beyond a certain age be required to take a test of cognitive competency? Should our nation impose term limits on Congress, as we have on the Presidency? Still, nothing has been done, and America is becoming weaker because of this issue. Here are some particulars.

Just a couple days ago, Republican Mitch McConnell, a co-leader of the US Senate was holding a press conference, and in the middle of his remarks, seemed to lose his place, and "freeze" while standing in front of the microphone, and saying nothing. This "dead air time" has been shown repeatedly in the news, raising questions on his health and fitness. News sources have revealed that he has fallen several times in the last year.

During the same week, Senator Diane Feinstein, a ninety year old democrat from California, launched into prepared remarks inappropriately in the middle of what was supposed to be a simple "yes/no" vote. News videos showed one of her aids leaning over and whispering instructions in her ear to, "just vote Aye!" She then complied. Still forgetting the distinction between debate and a yes/no vote is quite alarming. This forces the question, how old is too old?

Just a year ago, the deep blue state of Pennsylvania elected a man— Senator Fetterman, who had recently had a stroke. Fetterman had demonstrated what was referred to as "auditory processing" problems during a debate with his republican rival, but got elected anyway, despite an obvious brain impairment. After the election, news reports indicated that his impairment was much more severe than the public was told, and the man cannot put a coherent sentence together. It is literally painful to watch him on the tube trying to question a witness. This forces the question, how impaired is too impaired, when it comes to the governance of our country?

When these examples are coupled with the hilarious video footage (you can find this footage on You Tube), of our cognitively challenged president falling down multiple times, or tripping apparently on air, or losing his way when exiting a stage, or loosing his train of thought during prepared remarks, or even reading a teleprompter incorrectly (someone should really just tell him to never read the phrase "end of remarks" when it appears on the teleprompter). At this point, one has to ask why won't these aged dinosaurs ever retire? Can they not merely leave public service gracefully? Moreover, why does America continue to put these folks forward as leaders? Finally, and this is the most damaging question of all, in a very troubled world, where a war with China has been predicted by some in the US military, and where both Iran and North Korea are threatening to exercise their newly developed nuclear power, do we really want these incapable, cognitively limited people at the top of our national leadership?

On July 31, 2023, Newsmax republished some data from a story originally in the Washington Post, documenting the fact that our current Congress is "one of the oldest Congresses ever." Thus, today we have the most aged leadership in all of our history. This story is now gaining press attention, so much so that one satire article has appeared with the funny, yet probing title:

Is this an old folks home or the Senate chamber? 9 clues to look for!

One reason for this dilemma is the draw of exercising power. The power and prestige of these ruling positions in American Government provide such a strong, ongoing incentive that many politicians simply refuse to step down, as their age increases. These politicians simply talk themselves into believing that no "one could do the job better" and they persist in governance even in the face of obvious cognitive decline. Today, as I write this, America faces the prospect of a Presidential election in which the two candidates are both quite old (Trump who is 77 years old, vs. Biden, who is 80), and one—Biden-- has shown repeated signs of cognitive decline. Are these two, truly, the best America has to offer? Of course, no one has yet challenged the cognitive capacity of President Trump; he has not given any reason for anyone to challenge his capabilities. Still, age impacts everyone, and sometimes very subtly at first. Should there be a maximum age limit for someone running for President or Congress?

Dr. Ben Carson, another Black American leader I admire, and a former Secretary of Housing and Urban Development, has argued for both term limits and a required physical exam yearly which includes an assessment of mental status. In an interview with Newsmax on 8/1/23, he noted the mental impairments of Senators Feinstein and McConnell (mentioned previously) and correctly stated that the founding fathers never foresaw either an aging congress or that anyone would seriously want to remain in power for decades, as have these cognitively impaired leaders. That is the reason that the US Constitution did not include term limits, even for the Presidency, which is how Franklin D. Roosevelt managed to win the presidency in four separate elections in the 1930s and 1940s. It was only after that, that our country passed a term limit for the President. Still, why not such limits for all in power, including Congress and perhaps the Supreme Court?

Maybe (dare I hope) this is one issue in which both conservatives and liberals can agree—we need our best and brightest, our most experienced *seasoned men and women as national leaders; not our decrepit, cognitively limited who happen to be members of the right party in any given state. One might even hope that the politics of "falling" presidents, or incoherent congressional leaders may then become a thing of the past.*

REFLECTION 7:

Erase Our History? Why?

(written initially on 8/1/23)

W*ithin the last year or so, many statues of Confederate leaders have been taken down or removed, and military bases have been renamed, based on the delicate sensibilities of Black Americans. Within the last year, Fort Gordon in Georgia, Bragg in North Carolina, and Hood in Texas have all been renamed because those men, most of whom were high ranking, successful military men for the Confederacy, supported the losing cause in a war some 157 years ago. Statues of leaders like Generals Robert E. Lee or Nathan Bedford Forrest have been removed from court houses, and/or college campuses across the nation, and even from the grounds of state capitals in some southern states. Even President Lincoln's statue has been removed from some locations, which is interesting as he fought against slavery all his life, and led the Union during the Civil War. He was for the emancipation of slaves, and indeed signed the Emancipation Proclamation! Still, the "erase history" argument points out that he was quite prejudiced against Blacks generally, and did not believe in racial equality. Further, his vision was to ship the entire race back to Africa after the Civil War ended. Clearly any memory of this guy needs to go!*

In Georgia, one of our most used State Parks includes a massive mountain, Stone Mountain, in which is carved a base relief of three confederate leaders, Generals Robert E. Lee, Stonewall Jackson and Jeff

47

Davis, the President of the Confederacy. While that park is beloved by millions and has been visited by Blacks and Whites alike for many decades, some have argued that this massive stone artwork should be destroyed! The erasing of history knows no bounds.

Still, this movement involves much more than simply renaming military bases, destroying beloved artworks, or removing statues that various woke snowflakes find offensive. There has been an effort to actually rewrite history, in the form of the 1619 Project, which was launched in 2019— some 400 years after approximately 20 Black Slaves were imported into the colony of Virginia. The history curriculum which sprang from that was roundly criticized by historians from both the right and left of the political spectrum for outrageous claims. These ideas including such things as the "true founding" of America was the 1619 date, because that when slavery was introduced into the British colonies in America. Of course, that date ignores Native American history altogether, Viking settlements from the year 1000, along the Canadian coast, Spanish explorations of North America in the 1500s, as well as the founding of Jamestown in the Virginia colony in 1607, and the failed colony in North Carolina, which dated from 1587.

Another assertion of this curriculum was the proposition that one reason for the American Revolution was that the colonies wished to "protect" slavery in America and that the British were making an effort to end it. Historians have noted that this proposition was pure fiction. There was essentially no abolitionist movement in Britian in 1775 (when the fight at Concord Bridge and Lexington took place), or 1776 (when the Declaration of Independence was passed by Congress). Thus, this assertion is purely false, if not downright dishonest.

Many other points of inaccuracy have been noted in this "revisionist" history, and one can find a catalogue of them online. For now suffice it to say that biased academics can talk themselves into believing anything (e.g. a flat earth, eugenics, or critical race theory), and that some political ideologues choose their own narrative over history facts. Still, that leaves us with clear evidence of the woke left attempting to destroy, erase, or rewrite American history.

Now as one reflective point, I find nothing in the Bible about Jesus, ever attempting to rewrite history, so in general I cannot support this effort. Rather, Jesus embraced history throughout his ministry. He often quoted the "scriptures" (what we now call the Old Testament, which were, in his day, the only holy scriptures of the Jews), and that Book is nothing if not a well-respected history of the Jews and their God. Even King Saul, the first King if Israel, was not erased from the Old Testament, and one can make the argument that he should have been! After all, he tried to kill David, the next leader, beloved by God. When David assumed leadership, should he not have erased all history of King Saul? Suffice it to say he didn't.

Thus, from a biblical perspective, I'm at a loss as to why the woke crowd wants to rewrite or erase history. If indeed some things should be more emphasized in historical studies, one could make that point without having to argue to erase some history while increasing attention to other historic facts. Why doesn't the woke left take this erase history approach?

Further, even if someone found a justification for renaming various military bases or changing our history, one question is how far should we go? Should we rename Washington, DC, a city named after a known slaveholder? How about writing Tom Jefferson out of our American history? While he did write those wonderful, inspiration words "all men are created equal" he clearly owned slaves, and had a number of children by one of them. Shouldn't he be "cancelled" too? Where does one draw the line? This proposition of erasing history quickly enters the theatre of the absurd.

Next, from a tactical point of view, this movement to erase history, or make American history concentrate exclusively on slavery simply makes no sense. Again, if someone wants to suggest a new emphasis in history, as a former major in history myself, I'd support that move! I'm always interested in promoting new, challenging historical thought, and sometimes history should be revised to become more inclusive. Still, in making an effort to add *new thoughts to certain aspects of history, do not these woke activists realize they will need allies? If someone wanted to emphasize how slavery impacted history at specific times, does one really need to ignore other parts of history, and doesn't that "selective vision" simply make other potential allies, begin to fight against the effort?*

Finally, isn't it wise to remember history? If proponents of the idea that slavery played a much more important role in American history, should they not want to keep mementos of various Confederate leaders, if only to point to them while pointing out their flaws? It would seem that such a strategy would help accomplish their goals, more so than erasing history.

And that leads to another point. As someone who studies history and reads history, I have to note how often historical perspectives change. New information becomes available, and history is justifiably revised; that is the way of things. Sometimes revisions are painful for persons with cherished beliefs, but one thing is certain; it is always unwise, if not outright unfair to judge historical figures by standards and sensibilities of today. While we cherish the image of General G. Washington, we have to note how his behavior today would simply be considered criminal. Of course he owned slaves—he owned hundreds, but he also ordered a number of men publicly executed for desertion during the American Revolution. Those were, by and large, men who simply attempted to return home from the war because they were (1) unpaid, and (2) starving. Many leaders in all of America's wars prior to 1900 ordered men executed or flogged to the point of scaring. That was the practice of the period. This was common.

There are many non-military examples here. Various ministers, Preachers of the Gospel of Jesus Christ, ordered some 20 persons, mostly women, killed for witchcraft in Salem in the 1690s. Queen Elizabeth I of England ordered a number of persons burned alive, as did Bloody Mary, another English Queen. In today's world, should they be judged for that, based on today's standards of behavior? Of course not. Judging historical figures by the standards of today is simply stupid, on any level, and should never be done. Moreover, how will posterity judge us? What are we doing as common practice today that in 50 or 100 years will be viewed as utterly barbaric?

Still, I guess that we Conservative Christians will simply grin and bear it, while we wait. I really believe that when our country comes to its senses and elects someone who loves America (i.e. the awaited ouster of the Biden Crime Family), that all of these military bases will simply revert to their original names, by executive order. Further, while world-wide slavery is and was a historical abomination, I do respect many of the leaders who owned slaves. These men were the best men of their age, including Jeff Davis, Abe Lincoln, G. Washington, Thomas Jefferson, Gordon, U. S. Grant (another slave owner, by the way) and Nathan B. Forrest. For example, Robert E. Lee, was believed to be a true gentleman, a kind man, and a true American, even by his enemies (specifically both Lincoln and Grant)! It is true that Nathan Bedford Forrest was a slave owner and later, an early leader in the KKK, but it is likewise true that only five years later, he urged the disbanding of that same organization when he saw the original aims of that group corrupted. Any of those men were much, much better men than many of those that today's woke snowflakes wish to honor (e.g. various rap artists, Castro, Bill Clinton, Karl Marx, George Floyd, etc.). Here's an idea. If our nation once chose to honor those men, let's not destroy those statues, and dishonor those choices made by our ancestors, simply because of today's woke values. Let's leave our history alone!

Liberal Virtue Signaling: Hate has no home here! (unless you hate Trump, you have to hate Trump, and all white men, all Christians, and all other deplorables, and of course all republicans; that hatred is OK).

It has often been said that the wise take care in what they wish for. I'd add a corollary to that idea. Perhaps we should take care in who we honor. On occasion, one can see a statue of Martin Luther King around, and I like that. I have enjoyed standing reverently over that man's grave down in Sweet Auburn in Atlanta, just to reflect on his legacy. The man changed history, making this world a better place, because of his belief in

Jesus. He is an American leader that we should all honor. I'd like to see a few more statues of Jesus, or Gandi, Harriet Tubman, perhaps Nelson Mandella, and maybe a few others. Some of these were not American, but all should be honored; all were leaders who stood for non-violence, and by that, they created positive political change. These were men and women of integrity, of peace, who made a choice not be become victims. These men and women should always be among those we honor. With that in mind, instead of creating conflict by tearing down historic statues, wouldn't our time be better spent, building a few more?

We can probably all agree on some historic figures to honor. Rosa Parks comes to mind, as do the four black men who sat at a segregated dinner on February 1, in 1960 in Greensboro, NC. These persons, like those above, were not career criminals but rather were, by their actions, showing that they refused to be victims. All made our country stronger. I'd rather see America build more statues with these guys in mind, not tear down our past.

Postscript: In mid August, 2023, a group of native Americans filed suite to force or encourage a name change of the "Washington Commanders." That team had historically been named the "Washington Redskins," but in a bow to wokeness, the name was changed to Washington Commanders just several years ago—a much less compelling name. However, the new lawsuit states that the original name "Washington Redskins" was an honor to the warrior spirit of the Native American ancestors, and accurately reflected their warrior spirit and history. Thus, even minority groups are fighting against the wokeness of changing names to erase history. It's time to leave history alone.

A thought: By 2023 we can definitely conclude that the "go to time out" generation was not as successful at raising kids as the "beat your butt" generation.

REFLECTION 8:

The Trans Movement, LGBT, and Other Lies and Misnomers

(Written initially on 8/9/23)

I'd hate to pick up a beautiful woman in a bar one evening, and, later discover she had a penis. Call me old fashioned for that if you like, or sexist, or whatever, but really, who wants that type of surprise? Maybe, for that reason, I don't understand the "Push" for transgenderism today. I guess I just want people to be what they were born to be, and I really don't think folks should argue with their own biology. God created two sexes, not the myriad of imagined sexual deviations engendered in the term LGBT++ or whatever that term happens to be this week.

Even Disney, that woke, and soon to be dead entertainment company has gotten into the act on this one, by creating a new "Snow White" movie, one intended to be politically correct in every way! In this one, there is no "Snow White" since the actress playing that part isn't white. There is only one dwarf too, and I personally feel a bit shortchanged on that! In fact, it is clear that Disney remade that classic to be woke: to be politically correct in every way possible, by including all types of sexual preferences among those who, in the traditional flick, were identified as the "Seven dwarfs." What that company did create was more correctly labeled:

"Snow Brown and the Her, Him, They, Seven Diversity Hires."

And just for fun, here's another one.

I rear-ended a car this morning. The other driver got out and he was a dwarf. After looking at his car, he said, "I am not happy."

So, of course, I replied, "Which one are you then?" That's when the fight started…

Now you've heard the old adage "When the legend becomes fact, print the legend." That principle refers to legends that are not true, but have become widely believed. This is the world in which the democrats and the woke crowd now live. They have shouted so long and loudly that more than two sexes exist, that they now actually believe their own forceful propaganda. That is the very essence of stupidity. Further, they actually believe that a woman is not a woman, or that a man can become pregnant, and that gender is somehow "fluid." That's what they have talked themselves into believing; that's where they now live, at least in terms of human sexuality Of course, when they do their "gender reassignment" surgeries, they still have to choose between two choices: male and female. Do these people not think at all?

Now personally, I truly don't care who one wishes to make love with, or whom they wish to identify as. What I do care about is this; do not demand any longer that I agree with those idiotic beliefs, if I consider them morally wrong, stupid, ill-informed, or downright ignorant. After all, I have a right, in the USA, to believe what I wish to believe, and in those beliefs, I'm fairly traditional, and for two concrete reasons: First, I have a brain, and secondly, I use it.

It is a fact that only two biological sexes exist in the human species, as in virtually all other species on this planet. I understand that some species can transition from one sex to another, but humans cannot. Humans can talk themselves into believing a wide variety of things about themselves, but those beliefs, even if supported by "gender affirming surgery" and various medications, will not make those beliefs true. Still, any American has a right to "imagine into existence" any number of variations for themselves, and he or she can then pretend those variations exist, as long as they don't force a belief in those variations on me and others.

I have a right to believe that some sexual activity is wrong. Personally, I don't believe pedophilia, bestiality, or homosexuality are morally right, from a Biblical perspective. However, I am instructed not to judge others negatively for those beliefs, or for actions between consenting adults related to their beliefs. I also must note that our society has legal codes against some of these. Now these beliefs of mine should not be used as a reason to attack me. These beliefs do not make me a bad person. In fact it makes me fairly consistent with Christian thought and morality down through the ages. When it comes to sports, I'm finding myself coming down on the side of forcing men and women to compete athletically, with others of their biological gender. Males should compete with males and females with females, period; End of story. If men can compete in women's competitions, in swimming, or anything else, then they will have an advantage that is unfair to the biological women, some of whom have trained all their lives.

The news is filled every day with stories on advocates for trans-gender athletes, or conservatives pushing back against the woke idiocy of allowing biological men to compete with women. On July 8, 2023, Governor Gregg Abbot of Texas signed into law the "Protect Women's Sports Act," in Texas. That law mandates that biological men may not compete against women in various sports in that state. Two women competitors in women's sports, were on hand, and of course, were subject to very hateful speech by those on the woke left who were there to advocate for transgender persons. The protestors, of course, claimed to be protesting in the name of "love, inclusion, and tolerance" but in reality they shouted curses, threw objects, and spat, and did other hateful things to the young women who were there to celebrate this victory for women.

Now anyone with a mind can understand that a person, born a biological male who has the upper body strength and endurance of males, should not be allowed to merely announce that they are female and thereby compete in women's sports. Were that allowed, those biological men would win virtually every time. Further the women, many of whom have trained for a lifetime in order to compete in collegiate sports, would be at a significant disadvantage.

In another transgender related story today news outlets reported that shareholders are now suing Target stores for their "woke" pro-trans merchandising. It seems that, in a rather stupid bow to the woke left ideologies of trans genderism, Target had produced and marketed a line of clothes, including clothes for children, that were specifically designed to hide genitals of men who wished to identify as women. This was all part of their diversity and inclusion campaign, but of course, the general public reacted very negatively, so that campaign, like the previously mentioned Bud-Light marketing campaign, managed to lose significant market share for Target. The value of Target overall had decreased from 74 billion, to 60 billion! Damn right shareholders are filing legal actions! One can only say, thank God America is waking up to this insanity. This awakening of America is the exact opposite of "going woke!"

One final thought for trans folks, or LGBT++ or whatever name you are using this week. Most of us really don't care who you wish to sleep with, but we will insist that you do not cram your beliefs down our throat, or expect us to celebrate your personal sexual choices. That is called freedom, and if anything history shows freedom will not die easily, even when it is generally denied by a crooked department of injustice, a dishonest fbi, and a demented president. We are conservative Christians, and we choose to wake up and Let Freedom Ring!

One time before, America woke up. In 1775, at Concord Bridge, the British tried to take the arms from patriots, who got really pissed! In a few short years the British, the most powerful nation on the planet at that time, learned what it meant to lose.

American woke up again on December 7, 1941. Five years later we dominated the world.

In the last week of August, 2023, we saw for the first time a Mug shot of a former President of the United States. Our demented president Biden sent his woke-left cronies, his Soros funded prosecutors to make that happen during a Presidential election. With Trump ahead in the Republican Primary, this election interference is obvious. America is waking up again.

Of course, the infamous "Red Wave" failed to materialize in the last election, but another election IS coming. It should be interesting, this rousing of the sleeping Giant, this true America. Deplorables Will Arise! Many of us are really, really pissed. So until then, I'll write a few things and share these thoughts with a few friends.

Then, when it's time, I'll join my conservative friends on the battleline, and right along with them, I'll be saying…. "Hold My Beer!"

William N. Bender, Ph.D.

A Thought For Today: The left's boycott of a song made it a number one hit. The right's boycott of a beer cost the beer company 30 Billion. Now who, exactly has the power?

REFLECTION 9:

The Big Lie And Why I Believe it

(Written initially on November 19, 2022)

This reflection was actually written as a letter to my Congressman, Representative Andrew Clyde, a year ago. The democrats are, of course, the most dishonest group of hate-filled people on the face of the earth, and what they call the "Big Lie" is, in fact true. The "big Lie" is the belief that the last Presidential election (November, 2020) was stolen from President Trump and the American people. It was, and thus, the big lie is true. In short, I and any honest American really does believe what the democrats call the "Big Lie." Here is why.

Dear Congressman Clyde:

I enjoyed meeting you briefly at the concert in the Ritz in Toccoa, GA last night. As I mentioned my wife, Dr. Renet Bender, once taught at a satellite campus of Truett McConnell in Watkinsville, GA some 20 years ago, so we both have had "faculty wives" at that college. At that time, I was on the faculty of the University of Georgia, and we lived in Watkinsville, rather than Toccoa, GA. Also, as I said last evening, please tell your wife that she plays beautifully.

I'm sorry that I "recognized" you at an evening in which you were out to enjoy your wife's talent, and probably intended to be rather low key. At any rate, I did enjoy our brief "during the intermission" talk about politics. As I said, I'd been planning this letter for some time, and just this past week I was very pleased that Republicans captured the House this time around. Thus you, on the House Oversight Committee, can support investigations of some of the shameful antics of joe biden (the "big guy", who is apparently in for 10% of hunter's take of the millions from China, the Ukraine, and who knows where else). As I mentioned last evening, Congressman Newt Gingrich has previously called the bidens the biggest crime family in American politics, and I tend to believe that. As your constituent, I am looking forward to the investigations that we discussed, and here are several reasonable requests.

I'd request investigation of the "Hunter Laptop" story. Apparently the fbi (a crooked organization which can no longer be trusted, as it once gave Hillary a pass on destroying 30,000 emails which were under subpoena), made a biased effort to kill that story prior to the last Presidential election. In 2020, the fbi told zuckerburg at Facebook to downplay or eliminate that laptop story, as it was "Russian disinformation" WHILE THEY KNEW IT WAS TRUE! That story alone, had it been verified prior to the last Presidential election, could have swung the country against biden, and for Trump in such a close election. It is unacceptable in a supposed republic with a free press for any agency of the government to suggest what they know to be dishonest censorship to any information organization in this fashion and thus tilt a presidential election. Please investigate both the department of injustice, and the fbi (note the lower case letters here, a sign of my disrespect for them) for their extensive bias in the last election.

I would also like to have Zuckerburg and Facebook itself investigated. In 2020, Zuckerburg gave millions to a supposed non-profit which by regulation cannot engage in politics (I know this as I run a small non-profit myself; see thejohnbenderfoundation.org). Zuckerburg's non-profit was supposed to "get out the vote" in a non-biased fashion, but in fact millions and millions went to get out the vote in democratic districts and very few dollars went to Republican districts (such are the allegations I've seen on the news). This type of illegal use of non-profit funds can, and probably did swing the 19,000 votes in Wisconsin needed for Biden to win, or the 11,000 votes by which biden won Georgia. Those two states were critical to biden's win in 2020, and in both, the elections were biased, as noted above.

Based on these actions of the fbi, and zuckerburg's antics alone, it is reasonable to believe that these two events did, in fact, swing a Presidential election. These actions alone, if proven, can indicate that the 2020 Presidential election was "stolen." In short, I believe what the mainstream press calls the "big lie." If these allegations are true, then that big lie, is in fact true as well. I have no knowledge of voting machines that changed votes, or of the vote harvesting, or ballot box stuffing that has been alleged, but based on a crooked fbi and zuckerburg's actions, I do believe that the Presidential election in 2020 was stolen.

To put a timely point on this matter of extreme bias at the doj, just this morning as I read the news, I note that an investigation has been launched by the department of injustice of the "highly dangerous" ticketing problems in an upcoming pop concert (forgive my sarcasm here—I hope it gave you a laugh!). Imagine my surprise in Garland's choice to investigate that crap, and NOT investigate the biden laptop allegations, or the withdrawal from Afghanistan a year ago, or the lack of Presidential action to protect the Southern Border. The bias here is laughable, but also tragic; our government is not functioning in a fair and even handed manner.

I know that Congresswoman Green has introduced Articles of Impeachment against the President based on the inaction at the Southern Border. I request that you support that to the degree possible. Impeachment is an extreme measure, I know, but Trump was Impeached twice, and he did nothing wrong—he never committed any "high crime or misdemeanors." At this point I believe biden has, both by allowing his son to sell influence while he was a sitting vice president, and currently, by not enforcing the law and protecting our Southern Border. In short I want him impeached. Now I realize that democrats hold the edge in the senate, making impeachment a challenge, but is it unreasonable to hope that when presented with hard evidence, that one or two or maybe 10 or 12 of them might be honest enough to support an impeachment of biden? Of course that leaves a vice president taking the White House, and I trust her even less than biden, if that's possible. Still, biden, I believe has committed numerous high crimes and misdemeanors, and should be impeached.

I realize that you are a veteran, and while I am not, my Dad did fight for this country, and he taught us all to believe in America. I would like, some day, to once again believe in our nation, but the actions above cause any honest person pause in that regard. In fact, since the Obama administrations' weaponizing of the department of injustice, the fbi, and at that time the irs, I cannot say I've had faith in America. President Trump had us going in the right direction but that ceased when biden took office. Please help me; I want to believe in America again.

In closing, let me just say thanks for your service to our country, both in uniform, and today, and thanks for reading this "much too long" letter. As reward, I've enclosed herein a gift for you, a historic fiction novel which I wrote under the pen name, Jimmy Cherokee Waters. It is about the early settlement of your district in North Georgia, and begins in the Cherokee town of Tugaloo, which in the 1740s existed just outside of what is now Toccoa. The story traces the interactions of the Cherokee and early settlers, and carries through the Georgia Gold rush. The book is about 75% accurate to our history—I had to invent a few characters, but the battles once fought in your district are as accurate as I could make them given extant historical records. Anyway I hope you enjoy the read. I'm sure that, with your duties, it becomes quite a pleasure to read something not about current politics.

God Bless you, and thank you again.

Dr. William N. Bender

As blunt as I may seem, I really don't say half of what I'm thinking! Imagine if I did!

REFLECTION 10:

I Am a Black, Trans, Female, Revolutionary

9/24/23

I decided last January that I would begin to identify as a black trans, female. I want to get me some gov'ment benefets too!

I'll bet that reflection title above made you go, "Wait. What?" Here's the story. This past year, when my Sunday school class, of old white guys, was discussing New Year's resolutions, I awaited a pause and then announced that I was going to "Identify" this year, as a Black transgender female. I explained that I owned a house rental business and that I wanted the government benefits that flow to Black owned businesses and female owned businesses, and the headlines last year introduced me to the fact that anyone can identify as anyone else, regardless of the realities of sex, race, etc. Thus, I can "be" a black female, obtain all the advantages of that, and not have to actually "be" a black female! I thought the idea was grand, but my class informed me of the inherent dishonesty. They are Christians, after all. Oh well…

Still in an age where a man dressed as a woman can absolutely kill the highest selling name-brand beer, aren't we already through the looking glass here?

Did you hear the latest trans news about this coming Christmas? Rudolph changed his name to Rolonda, and is now winning all the female reindeer games!

So much for being a black trans female. Guess it's just not in the cards for me. Now the revolutionary part, I still wonder about. In fact, there are serious discussions on questions like, "Is a Civil War coming to America?" This of course, begs the question, what war in all history was ever civil? Sorry, I am a wordsmith, a writer by nature, and I like to play with words. Still here goes.

Is a revolution coming? YES.

When? WITHIN THE NEXT TWO YEARS.

What is the evidence for that conclusion? WE'LL START WITH HISTORY.

Remember the infamous "Shot heard around the world?" That phrase originated with a poem in 1837, referring to first rifle fire of the American Revolution. The shot was probably fired in Lexington, but is often associated with Concord Bridge, and it may have started the American Revolution. Nobody knows who fired that shot (or even if it was fired on Concord Bridge, or a bit earlier that same day on Lexington Green). What we do know is that the shot was fired in April of 1775, well before the Declaration of Independence committed the American colonies to war. Most folks don't realize that the American Revolution (the shooting war) actually began before before the signing of the Declaration of Independence.

Today we celebrate July 4 when the Declaration of Independence was signed as the beginning of America, but it is a fact that blood was already shed well before that day. One wonders, did those 82 American Patriots lined up on Lexington Green know they were beginning a revolution? They were pissed off, but did they really mean to go to war?

Further, it is well documented that long after that shot was fired, many leaders in the Second American Continental Congress did not want a war with Great Britian. Clearly those men in Philadelphia didn't believe they were already in a war for independence. In fact, the next battles in that war—The Battle of Bunker Hill (which was really fought on neighboring Breed's Hill, near Boston) was also fought well before the war began with the Declaration of Independence.

If we go further back before those fights, we find that the "Boston Massacre" which led to the deaths of five patriots, happened five years before the Lexington Green battle. Going further back, some historians have suggested that the American Revolution really began with the "Regulator War" in Alamance, North Carolina in 1771. That battle was, perhaps the first time blood was shed on the North American continent in an effort to demand regulation for the dishonest taxmen, judges, and officials in the upper reaches of the Carolina Colony. Clearly, when a government is crooked, pissed off patriots are often ready to go to war. In that "Regulator" fight in North Carolina, about 1000 patriots lined up and opened fire on a slightly larger group of "The King's Forces." Did our American Revolution really begin there?

The lesson here is clear. History shows us that revolutions begin before any one realizes it, and I believe the next one is here, or at the very least, on the way.

As to a coming revolution, we now have our government preparing to take weapons from the populace, just as the King's men were doing when they marched to Concord and Lexington, where they believed tons of gunpowder and shot were being stored. We have excessive taxes used for anything and everything the progressive left wants (help for illegal aliens, sending uncounted monies to wars elsewhere, paying and arming irs agents) while our nations' veterans are ignored, and infrastructure needs forgotten. Further, the government caused inflation of the last two years is merely a "hidden tax" on all Americans, and most of those funds are used for leftist causes like forgiveness of student debt, dishonest green energy policies, support for illegal aliens (migrants), or other pet causes of the left. Like many deplorable Americans, I'm pissed off about that.

I've already noted here in the Diary that excellent documentation exists that our president, demented though he is, has been dishonest as hell for most of his years in government, enriching himself at my expense, and as of this week (August 28, 2023), he is now facing a serious impeachment inquiry in Congress because of his illegal activities.

Lately, he has done the unthinkable—something never before done in American politics.

Biden and his Soros funded cronies have indicted his main political opposition—President Trump, in an attempt to use dishonest, untrue charges, and a crooked court system, a crooked fbi, and a crooked doj, to eliminate political opposition. This is truly third world stuff, an unimaginable act if ever there was one. Even Nixon, another dishonest president, never attempted to have his political opposition arrested! Again, we are through the looking glass, and any expectations of "normal" or "fair" government today are misguided.

Now I should note that we are two years past the supposed January 6 "Insurrection." The dishonest democrats would have one believe that our government was about to fall because a couple hundred patriots had had enough of the dishonesties, and entered the US Capital illegally. Supposedly this "insurrection" was an attempt to over turn the US presidential election of 2020. As I've mentioned before, that election was "stolen" and I do believe the facts suggesting that it was bought and paid for by dishonesties of the left. But it is time to get real here. The January 6, 2021 capital riot was no more an insurrection than was the Million Man March of a few years ago. I mean, the rioters, the few who were armed, had left their stash of guns in a hotel in another state, for God's sake. They did break down some barriers to get into the building, but once there, they didn't destroy anything, didn't burn anything. They were basically escorted around by the Capital police! If this was in insurrection, it was the worst insurrection in history, and the video shows that!

Still, there is much historical precedent here. The Storming of the Bastille (a large government prison in France which was overtaken by French Patriots on July 14, 1789), took place well before anyone was talking about a revolution. Still, that day turned out to be the beginning of the French Revolution. Those hungry peasants who took over that prison didn't realize they were starting a revolution—they just wanted something to eat. Also, they were really pissed off at a corrupt government that ignored their hunger, and in more general terms, ignored the will of the people.

Does this sound familiar? Is this happening in America today? Haven't some 81 million Americans who voted for Trump been labeled deplorable by the democrats? Is such infantile name calling really the highest form of political debate for the democrats? Haven't our thoughts and wishes been ignored (if not criminalized) by our government? When every conservative opinion is labeled "racist" or "hate speech" aren't we already living in a dishonest world? Such things ultimately cause revolutions, my friend, and that is historic fact.

Three things create revolutions; hunger, high taxes, and dishonest governments. In our case, two out of three ain't bad!

With that noted, many of those men who rioted at the Capitol on January 6, 2021, have now received a crooked trial, and resulting prison sentences of months, years, or decades. I should note that the video that shows essentially no "insurrection" was withheld from their defense attorneys for those patriots now serving jail time. This is truly third world stuff—I'd expect such withholding of "important exculpatory evidence" in China, Russia, or North Korea, but in an American courtroom? Never! Those guys were clearly denied a fair trial, and they are now in prison! On this basis, our corrupt fbi or doj can arrest anybody, withhold evidence, and toss anyone in jail. After an unfair trial, they'll keep you there, in jail, for 20 years or so.

You might recall Trump's famous claim: "They aren't just coming for me; they are coming for you." I believe that. You should too.

Of course, I'm still waiting to hear how long the sentences are for the blacks and whites that burned down the six blocks of downtown Seattle a couple years ago. When will those antifa leftists be sentenced? Funny, I guess, but I'm not holding my breath. Our dishonest fbi, doj, and federal government does not act against rioters on the left of the political spectrum, only those deplorables like me, who are conservative. This is a crooked, dishonest government. Such governments breed revolutions.

Still, you want actual evidence that a revolution is coming? Here's a few more things that make me think a real, blood in the streets revolution is on the horizon, perhaps within the next year or two.

First, as I pointed out above, revolutions tend to begin before anyone knows they have begun. Our first one began sometime between 1771 and 1775, but wasn't actually recognized until July 4, 1776. It is not unrealistic to think that the next revolution has already begun.

Second, our government agencies have been corrupted, and now serve only one political party—the dishonest democrats. The 81 million Americans who voted for Trump, we deplorables, should expect no justice from this government once we are arrested. The January 6 rioters got no justice. We should expect none. Most of us will not tolerate that for long.

Next, President Trump's mug shot is now on a T-shirt. This is a first in US history. Now, I'm going to have to get me one of those shirts. It will be part of the patriot uniform, I think for this coming revolution. Biden and the democrats are attempting to use the courts to eliminate political opposition. That has never happened in America, and no democracy can tolerate that.

Next, recent elections have been stolen, by leftist funding that should have been neutral but wasn't. I wrote about what the democrats call the Big Lie, earlier. I believe that "big lie."

Next, our current president is both demented and crooked as a snake in the grass. He should be impeached, and soon will be. That alone could begin things.

Next, some people have already been arrested for the Jan 6 non-insurrection. Clearly there are patriots out there who are as angry as I am. Those men, now in jail, are our Lexington Green Militia. May God Bless Them!

Next, this shows that political opposition, other than merely Trump, are being arrested.

Next, our right of free speech is being silenced by the government colluding illegally with big tech. Several federal judges have stated that in judicial decisions. Clearly our government, well beyond the biden crime family, is quite corrupt.

Next, the leftists are most insistent on taking weapons from the American people regardless of the US Constitution. This was also the reason for the fight at Lexington and Concord Bridge. I'll happily stand in the shadow of those patriots of long ago, shouting with my brothers,

"You can take my gun, when you pry my cold, dead fingers from around the barrel!"

Next, these idiots in power are talking again about vaccinations (remember all the vaccines that didn't work at all the first time?), and even mask mandates. Are they that stupid (well, yes)? Do they really want to control us that badly (again, Yes)?

Next, we have another presidential election coming, and if the last election is any indication, the next election will be stolen also.

Next, various polls show Trump is leading Biden in a head to head matchup. One poll came out September 24, 2023, from a democratic leaning organization, the Washington Post. It showed that Trump was leading Biden in a head to head matchup by 10 points!

Next, dishonest leftists will not tolerate a Trump win. Should that happen, they will make every attempt to make sure Trump is not elected, or if so, is not allowed to take office. Tucker Carlson has openly predicted that, since two impeachments didn't silence Trump, and four indictments haven't silenced Trump, the next thing on the horizon is Trump's assassination.

And that's when the revolution begins.

I would love to be wrong, and I sincerely mean that. I'll say it again; I would love to be wrong. Sometimes I am wrong. Still, I do have a brain, and I have learned to use it. Just look again at the list above. Read that list again. It should scare the hell out of you. It scares me.

Clearly within two years, all of these things will come to a head, one way or another.

To review, the first American Revolution may have begun with the Regulator War in NC in 1771, or the Boston Massacre of 1771, or at Lexington Green, in 1775, or at Bunker Hill in 1775. All of that happened before the Declaration of Independence and subsequent birth of our nation. Both our Revolution and the French Revolution began before people realized it. History tells us that revolutions generally begin before anyone sees what is coming.

Again, I truly believe in this country's Constitution, in our freedoms as guaranteed within that constitution, and moreover in the noble experiment of America itself. However, no one can seriously believe that what we have now is the government of the US Constitution--a dishonest president taking bribes to sell influence, a one-sided use of the courts, dishonest prosecutors choosing when to apply the law, a dishonest fbi, doj, irs, and who knows what else, a silenced (they hope) populace, attempted controlled by mask mandates, and like 2021, limited public gatherings, attempted gun control, and election interference via "trumped up" Trump charges. Is this the government delineated by the US Constitution? Is this the government we were promised in America? Really?

Well, the next 24 months promise to be interesting. For me, like old Patrick Henry said:

Give Me Liberty or, well, you know, you know, the thing....

Sorry. I was channeling our demented President there. Sounded just like slow joe, didn't it? When I'm worried, my humor overcomes me. Then again, I might as well indulge it a bit. After all, I believe I mentioned that I'm a trans, black female, and this reflection shows, I'm probably a Revolutionary as well.

When it all begins, when the battle lines are drawn, and guns are being loaded, you'll find me beside my conservative Christian brothers— standing in the tradition of the Regulator War of the Carolinas. I'll be right there, right on the next Concord Bridge, or at Lexington Green, or Bunker Hill. You'll see me there—I'll stick out in a crowd. I'll be the only trans, black female Patriot wearing a Trump Mug Shot T Shirt!

REFLECTION 11:

Sex, Race, and Black Crime Don't Exist
9/27/23

B efore I begin, I should note that I'm off the trans, black female thing for now, just so you know my frame of reference here. Still, just today, I discovered that Sex did not exist!

Now I remember being a very "energetic" 15 year old boy with all the hormones that those years entail, so imagine my surprise to find out I'd been mislead all along! I actually thought two sexes existed! In fact, I planned much of my life around that belief! I thought sex was a fairly important thing. Imagine that!

Still, just this morning I saw a relatively obscure news item about a scholarly conference that cancelled a panel discussion about biological sex. The organizations putting on that conference thought that such a discussion might "offend" the LGBT (and whatever other letters they use this week) folks. The story was reported in the Daily Caller, a conservative news outlet I generally trust. It stated that an Anthropology Conference had cancelled a previously scheduled discussion that focused on how the field of anthropology research in general was dependent on using sex in anthropological research. That scientific field simply has to focus on sex to do any serious research, and such science is based on the reality that there are two biological sexes among humans and all of the animal kingdom.

When an anthropologist initially digs up a human skeleton, one of the first questions involves sex differences between male and female bones. In analyzing ancient remains it is often important to know if a set of human remains belonged to a King in ancient times or a Queen. Hard to do anthropology without those data, but in today's world, such facts might offend someone. Therefore, sex does not exist, right? At least not in the form of two biological sexes.

In fact, discussions of sex might offend the skeleton itself, who might have been a "he, she, them LGBT-IDIOT" ten or fifteen centuries ago! May God forgive us if we offend those bones by assigned them one of two biological sexes that, by today's standards, do not exist. Even worse, we might use incorrect pronouns! No doubt some other LGBT-IDIOT will immediately demand reparations again for such cruel, harsh treatment! (Sorry for my play with letters there, but I couldn't help myself). But here's the worst truth of all.

We are so far into never, never land today that scientific inquiry now has to be sacrificed at the alter of political correctness.

Now I've been a scientist and a researcher in human behavior. I've written and published about 60 peer reviewed articles over the years in scholarly journals. I've presented articles and papers; I've done panel discussions at scores of conferences and done many hundreds of professional workshops. I can tell you for a fact, that a panel discussion at a scholarly conference is generally as edge-of-seat exciting as a rerun of Lassie, or last year's America's Cup. Boring doesn't nearly cover it. Still, in today's world, the apparent belief is that all of us must change our behavior, and apparently even compromise our academic integrity and scientific inquiry, so as not to offend anyone, who may have deluded themselves into believing in more than two biological sexes. Thus, a scholarly discussion that would probably have shown how important sexual identification of human remains is, in the field of anthropology, cannot now be held. This is the level of stupidity, of sheer dishonesty, demanded by the LGBT-IDIOTS of the ever-politically correct, left.

I pointed out previously in this Diary, that evil wins if honest folks remain silent, and that I was no longer going to remain so. Therefore, I'll state it bluntly then. Cancelling this panel discussion, that no one would have ever heard about anyway, was the dumbest thing they could have done. Frankly, I want our society to proceed with all haste in almost every scientific arena, and that includes accurate, honest, anthropology, and stating that there are really only two biological sexes is a simple fact on which scholarly inquiry in that particular field depends. If you give up that reality, you are left with virtually nothing to gain from scholarly inquiry into the past. Further, if that fact offends someone, then we might wish them well and hope that they one day grow up. We simply cannot allow such liberal, leftist dishonesty to stand, if it compromises honest academic inquiry.

I'm going to print up a T Shirt one day. It will say: I raised a liberal. I'm sorry!

In a broader sense though, I have to note several other unpleasant facts that, because they might have offended someone, are never discussed. In fact, even conservative media intentionally hide much important information that might offend someone, and here's an example, again from the headlines today.

Fox News, Newsmax, and even CNN presented a story this morning on 100 teens who looted several stores in Philadelphia last night (9/26/23). Some news outlets suggested the teens looted as a response to a judge's decision to dismiss charges against a white cop who shot a black perpetrator. Approximately 20 arrests were made during and after the looting. As is consistent with all news outlets, none of these sources reported on the race of the perpetrators who were arrested. Why leave out that part of the story, a story in which race was very much a factor?

When I read those versions of the same story, I mentioned to my wife that most inner city crime is committed by those who live in inner cities, and much of it by blacks because that's where many Blacks live. I'd like to know the race of those perpetrators, because it might be important in understanding that story. Further, there was some video footage of these crimes. That could have been presented in the news, or the racial mix of those arrested could have been reported, both of which were important parts of the story. Still, in today's politically correct world, I was denied that information, because journalistic practice has long suggested that racial information about a perpetrator or perpetrators might offend someone. It might show that blacks commit crimes! Imagine that! This is clearly dishonest journalism—to have relevant information and withhold it.

For decades now, it has been considered "racist" to even point out when a large percentage of perpetrators belong to minority groups, and someone can get "cancelled" if not drawn and quartered for even discussing the fact that a plethora of crime statistics indicate that blacks, based on percentage of the population, commit more crimes than whites. This is why blacks, who make up approximately 13% of the American population, comprise approximately 33% of the populations in our jails and prisons (these are facts; look it up, folks). That fact alone makes the race of suspected perpetrators relevant in news stories such as this, but once again, our society is lying to itself by excluding this information from such news stories. Just for the sake of honesty, here are the percentage figures for prisoners in the USA today.

Race	% of US Population	% of Prison Population
White	*59%*	*30%*
Black	*13%*	*33%*
Hispanic	*19%*	*23%*
Asian	*6%*	*1.8%*
Native American/Alaskan	*2.9%*	*2.3%*

These data show that blackness alone is not a factor in terms of who goes to prison. Were being black a causal factor here, then blacks would presumably be the only group where the percent of incarcerations outdistance the percent of the population, and that is not the case here. In fact, in two of these racial groups, the percentage of prisoners is higher than one would anticipate. Thus, there is some "cause" for this, other than race itself.

Of course, various black leaders like Larry Elder, Dr. T. Sowell, and others have pointed out the same disproportionate rate of incarceration for blacks, as that noted here, and they are honest enough to point to the real reason for this. Neither they, nor I believe that any "racial genetic cause" creates more black criminals. Like these gentlemen, I believe that this racial disparity in our prisons is probably related to higher rates of fatherlessness in the black community today. Today 70% of black kids are raised in a home without a father. That is the problem we must, sooner or later discuss seriously, as a society. Honesty demands such a discussion, before we lose our inner cities entirely. Still, today, I am denied information relevant to particular news items, because such information might offend somebody. This dishonesty, via refusal to report important, available information that will help citizens interpret news stories is unacceptable. So here's a simple reality.

Even if the truth hurts someone's feelings, it is still the truth!

Now someone one the left might argue that reporting on perpetrators' race, when so many perpetrators seem to be disproportionately black or Hispanic, may lead our country towards racism! There's that catch all term again! Of course, according to the dishonest left, all white people are racist anyway, and blacks or Hispanics, etc. cannot be racist. Now that line of argument is pure BS in the most evident way.

Deju Moo: The feeling that I've experienced this same bullshit before!

Still, here's the real problem with not reporting on the race of perpetrators honestly: this hiding of the truth, this denial of information also effectively prohibits our society the means to hold any discussion about what to do to fix the problem. Without honestly showing how large the problem of black crime is in America, virtually no one is talking about it, except for those Black leaders mentioned above and a couple others; Larry Elder, Tim Scott,

Candice Owen, and Dr. T Sowell. These persons have repeatedly pointed to fatherlessness in the black community as the problem, leading to ill-disciplined kids, and criminal behavior in teens and young adults. Unless we address fatherlessness in our nation, we will simply put, not survive the wave of crime that is growing ever larger. Our inner cities will become wastelands—many have already—and riotous gangs of various races will continue to "flash Mob" and loot community stores and commit other crimes at will. These black leaders believe fatherlessness is the issue; so do I.

And here's a second problem the left doesn't want to talk about. Most black crime is committed against black victims! While anyone's store can—apparently—be looted today and most of the criminals will get away free, it is a fact that most victims of black crimes are black themselves. People tend to commit crime in their own neighborhoods, and those inner city neighborhoods are already wastelands. In that sense our police, courts, and society in general are failing our black citizens. I wish the left ideologues were honest enough, or cared enough, to look at the real problems here. I wish they would allow an honest discussion of those problems, but honesty is an anathema to democrats and liberals. These people simple cancel any facts they don't like.

If you want to see how other good ideas that have racial overtones can be "cancelled" by political correctness in our culture, look up "SuperPredator" on Wikipedia. The idea of the superpredator is that increasingly impulsive youth, often raised in inner cities, frequently commit crime without remorse—they thus become superpredators. The idea was politically incorrect so it has been attacked and is now called a "myth." It is regarded as a "Myth," mainly because it led to increased incarceration of blacks, suggesting that race is one consideration in analysis of violent crimes in the 1980s and 1990s. This term offended the left, so the truth of the superpredator idea is now regarded as a myth.

Personally, I still consider that superpredator idea valid. The inner city youth in these "flash mob" crimes are impulsive, and commit crime apparently without remorse. Thus, the idea of the superpredator is a "myth" *in the same sense as other" myths" the left doesn't like. Here are a few more "myths," all of which have, ultimately been shown to be true.*

Blacks and Hispanics, on a percentage basis, commit more crimes than other racial groups. This is probably associated with poverty, and is certainly related to fatherlessness.

The Covid virus came from a lab leak at a poorly run lab in China.

Development of the Covid virus was funded by American tax dollars.

The Hunter Biden laptop was real, as were the emails it contained that implicated President biden in various crimes such as bribery or extortion.

Russia did not collude with Trump in the Presidential race of 2016. Trump won that race fair and square.

Hillary Clinton DID collude with Russia in 2015 and 2016. Her campaign funded and used Russian sources to develop the informational lies used against Trump; the falsehood that Trump colluded with Russia!

Congressman Schiff from California is a flat-out liar. He knew the "Russia collusion" allegations against Trump were lies, and he pushed them anyway for well over a year.

The fbi, doj, and irs are extremely politically biased against conservatives.

Catholics, Christians, whites, conservatives, and parents at PTA meetings are, generally speaking, neither racists nor terrorists, even though our own government has so labeled us.

Trump took a few papers home when he left office, just like biden, Pence, and many other national leaders have done. Trump's home was the only one raided by the fbi. This shows a biased, two tier, system of justice that operates against conservatives.

Our federal government is corrupt.

Jow biden. our president takes bribes totaling millions and millions of dollars.

Most of the national media in America today, serves as a mouthpiece for the democrats, and leans so far to the left it is a wonder they can stand upright.

The event on January 6, 2021 at the capital was a riot, not an insurrection.

Again, all of these things have been identified as "untrue" by today's national media, and all are true. Here's a couple more truths.

There really are only two biological sexes.

Race is a factor in who commits crime in our nation today. Therefore, the race of suspected perpetrators and victims should always be reported by the news outlets.

We can only hope that one day, at some distant point in the future, some news outlet will pay attention to the old adage from Dragnet.

We want the truth, the whole truth, and nothing but the truth.

I hope to live to see that day.

Postscript: On September 28, 2023, several combined committees in the United States Congress, began joint meetings focused on evidence for impeaching Joe biden. Unlike the two times President Trump was impeached (he was never convicted), there is actual evidence which shows that biden actually committed various crimes.

REFLECTION 12:

Secession! It Can Happen Again!

I've commented on a wide number of news items, from a conservative Christian perspective, but I haven't mentioned the ongoing secession movements around the USA. Recently I watched a you tube video by Dr. Turley and another clip from the Christian Broadcast Network on Secession movements in the news today! Now the last time secession was seriously tried in the USA, it did not work out too well. It led to the War Between the States in 1861. When 11 states decided that they could not tolerate their property rights (i.e. slaves) being taken by the federal government with Abe Lincoln as President, they opted to quite the USA. Moreover, they should have been allowed to do so! Nothing in the US Constitution says that once a state has entered into that Union, that it cannot walk away at any point in the future. Technically, those states should have been allowed to just "walk away" and form, in their mind at least, a more perfect union.

Oh, well. That didn't happen, and consequences of that secession movement were horrendous—the South lost a war to defend the rights of states to govern themselves (even though that was the express purpose of the US Constitution), and ultimately the entire Confederacy was turned into a bastard step child of the Union. The South remained something of a "colony" of the Union states, for nearly 100 years—with major resources in the South exploited by Union business interests.

One can always play "what if" games in history. What if the Confederates had won that war? Would slavery still exist (Probably not, since it was likely to fail when the cotton crop did). Would we have ever implemented a federal income tax? Would we now have a draconian federal government ever reaching into the pockets of Americans with increased taxes, and increasingly taking away the rights that are assured us in the US Constitution? In spite of the slavery then practiced in the Confederacy, and in a few Union states in 1861, maybe the "states rights" idea wasn't such a bad one. The framers of the US Constitution didn't think so—they did virtually everything possible to protect the rights of states to govern themselves. Well, I know it is politically incorrect to point that out, but, well, I like to be honest. I'm strange that way.

My Life Coach just informed me that I didn't make the team!

In headlines today we can see that secession, in a slightly different form, seems to be happening again. As I say, I've seen several news stories about it. For example, the Christian Broadcast Network reported on the 12 counties in Oregon that have already voted to succeed from Oregon and join Idaho. This is called the "Greater Idaho Movement." In Oregon, there are really two states. Portland—a deep blue city dominates the coastal region, and it is a bastion of crime, drug addiction, homelessness, and "defund the cops" movement. In short, it is a nightmare, just like other deep blue democratic cities around the nation, Philadelphia, Detroit, New Orleans, San Francisco, Denver, Boston, Washington, DC, Seattle, Atlanta, and New York, to name a few! All are controlled by democrats and, as a result, none are fit places to live any more. My wife and I have decided not to travel to any of these places, simply because they are not safe.

But back to Oregon. While Portland dominates the western part of the state, across the Cascade Mountains that cut Oregon in two, the eastern part of the state is deeply conservative. Those counties want a government that represents them, so they want to split and join a conservative state next door, Idaho. The CBN story showed how Christians in eastern Oregon found that the woke, leftist social agenda forced on them by the state leaders in Portland *was more than offensive—they believed the ultra-liberal policies on gender identity issues, gun control, and abortion were actually anti-Christian. They are right. So there's the question. Why should they have to stay in a state that doesn't represent their values?*

I hope that the Greater Idaho Movement succeeds eventually, though I think it is quite unlikely. The liberal, dishonest democrats who are in power in Oregon, will fight this tooth and nail! In contrast, Idaho has generally supported this, with non-binding resolutions being passed for engaging in "talks" about changing the state border. In some cases in the past, state borders have been changed. Still, Oregon, dominated by liberal democrats, shows little interest in such discussions.

Again, I'd personally love for this secession idea to catch on. In fact, I'd like the same thing to happen in Georgia. In my state, the cancer that is Atlanta (very blue, very liberal) is completely out of step with almost all the rest of Georgia, and I'd love to see our conservative counties succeed and join neighboring Alabama, Tennessee, or South Carolina. If it could happen in Oregon, why not in Georgia? Maybe other conservative states that are dominated by liberal—deep blue cities, should consider a similar movement.

In fact, the CBN reported that a number of states have considered secession movements similar to Oregon. In New York, the upstate feels "dominated" by New York city politics and has seen the introduction of secessionist legislation. In Michigan, the upper peninsula has considered becoming its own state, as they feel they are not at all similar to Detroit. Other states with similar issues include California, Washington, Colorado, New Mexico, and Maryland. Many of those are dominated by politics in deep blue cities (e.g. Seatle in Washington, and Denver in Colorado), while most of the rural counties elsewhere are quite conservative.

Just as a thought: how many more conservative republican Senators would there be, if all of those secession movements succeeded? Maybe 8? Maybe 10? We'd definitely see a changed federal government if that happened!

Texas is another example, but with a slightly different twist; It is the only state in the Union that is assured of the right to subdivide itself. Unlike every other state, Texas fought a war for its own independence (from Mexico in 1836; Remember the Alamo!) and Texas won! Texas was its own country from 1836 until 1845, when it joined the USA. Because of that decision in 1845, Texas is guaranteed the right to subdivide itself, should they choose to do so, into as many as five states. It is interesting to contemplate that possibility, though I doubt Texans would consider such a move. Still, if they did subdivide into 5 states, the deep blue cities of Dallas, Houston, and Austin would control at least one and perhaps two of those new states. That means that three new states would be primarily republican, and that alone would swing the Senate into the Republican camp! That would be wonderful! We'd then have a Republican House, and a Republican Senate, and only our demented president would stand in the way of making our country great again!

I've decided to support the LGBTQ Movement! Let's Get Biden To Quit!

As I understand it from the CBN news video, for a state border to be moved, two state legislatures have to agree to the move, and then, the US Congress has to approve that move. This makes these secession movements highly unlikely to succeed. Still, this might be possible, if enough persons find it to be to their own advantage. The secession movement in Oregon, for example, has pointed out that should the liberal state leadership in Portland allow them to move their conservative counties to Idaho, then the "new" Oregon would not have to contend with so much conservative disagreement. Thus, it might be an advantage to the liberals in Portland to simply "let my people go!"

From a more practical point of view, even conservatives have a right to a government that reflects their values—that is the whole reason behind the "states rights" argument to begin with. Why should conservatives be forced into states that do not represent their values?

As our nation's politics heat up (I've discussed the reasons for that in *Diary of a Deplorable* earlier) it will be interesting to watch these various movements from state to state. Once again, I'm pulling for the underdog here. I mean, isn't that what Christians are all about anyway?

Dr. William Bender

Afterword: I've heard that a fairly large number of folks are now reading and sharing these copies of the *Diary of a Deplorable*. I'm glad of that and hope it makes you think and laugh a bit. To make this more available, I'll be sending this out from now on to a new email list, and I'm inviting anyone and everyone to sign up to get those emails. Just send a brief message to me: ***benderbilly53@gmail.com*** and I'll add you to the list. Please share all of these reflections with like minded folks, and invite them to join the email list. Thanks. I hope this makes a difference.

REFLECTION 13:

Democrats Can't Break Laws

William N. Bender, Ph.D.

*L*ast week, as the US House of Representatives debated a budget resolution to keep our government functioning, a Black member of the House decided to obstruct the proceedings of that governing body. He pulled a fire alarm to force evacuation of one of the office buildings that house members of the House. If you've watched the news within the last week, you've probably seen the video of that crime taking place. Like most conservatives, I'm still waiting, probably in vain, for him to be charged with a crime. This leads to the obvious conclusion;

Democrats Can't Break Laws.

Let's just go ahead and admit that democrats, liberals, and woke ideologues can't break laws. That is to say, the law doesn't apply to them, so they can't break the law. This is saying the same as they can break any law they choose, because the law doesn't apply. Today, in the USA the law only applies to you if you are a conservative. If we admit that, then our current system of injustice makes sense. Conservative Republicans are the only persons that the crooked doj will investigate, and the injustice department will prosecute—thus democrats can't break the law! It doesn't exist for them.

A number of national leaders, including President Trump, have noted that this obstruction charge, the law broken by that black member

85

of the US House of Representatives, was exactly the same charge that was levied against the rioters from the January 6, 2021 capital riot. A large number of conservative persons have been charged with that obstruction charge, and so it would seem very reasonable to file that charge against the Black Congressman—I'm not using his name because he is just another unimportant liberal overall. He's just an "oppressed" black man fighting desperately for what he knows is right—at least that is how liberals will portray him. But of course, as noted above, democrats can't break laws, since no laws apply to them. Still, he actually did the same crime as a number of very patriotic persons who have now been sentenced for 18 or 20 years in the pen for obstruction of the governing body—the US House and Senate. When will he be charged with that crime? Again, we have to conclude that democrats can't break laws.

It is a sorry shame that in the USA today, conservatives can only expect a two tier system of justice. When a conservative does a crime, the entire weight of the federal government operates against him! The injustice department, the irs, and the dishonest fbi—all collude to put conservatives in jail, just like they are now doing against President Trump. They will be coming for you and me next; while I'm fairly unimportant, so were many of those prosecuted after the January 6 riot.

However, when a democrat breaks the law, he or she gets a "pass!" We can only remember that Hillary Clinton—another dishonest democrat—intentionally destroyed over 30,000 emails WHILE THOSE MESSAGES WERE UNDER SUBPOENA!

Hillary, because she was a liberal democrat, was then given a "pass" by the fbi director comey, who decided not to prosecute her. Hillary was, of course, a democrat. This represents multiple times democrats should have faced justice but didn't, while conservative republicans are skewered by the various agencies of our dishonest federal government.

And since we are going back in history a bit, let's not forget old bill Clinton himself, another democrat liberal. The man was impeached for lying to the American public, which he did, but the dishonest democrats in the Senate did not vote for impeachment, so he was not removed from office. What was proven was that after he said on television that He "did not have sex with that woman" it was shown that he did in fact "have sex with that woman!" He finally had to admit that in a televised interview. I mean, the man got oral sex in the oval office, for God sake!

Just makes you so proud to be an American! You just want to shout, "Way to Go, Bill!"

OK. That was sarcasm (my sense of humor again). There is absolutely nothing about either bill or Hillary that makes me proud. They are like most democrats in their incredible dishonesty and hypocrisy, and together they have reduced the office of the Presidency. Now Bill was impeached for those lies about his sexual exploits, but again, the democratic controlled Senate did not find him guilty, EVEN THOUGH HIS GUILT WAS CLEARLY ESTABISHED!

So again, we see that democrats who are clearly guilty of crimes are not held accountable; democrats can't break laws. This list could go on and on—remember that Trump's home was raided by the fbi for holding onto top secret documents. Biden likewise held on to top secret documents, storing them in several homes and a garage, but there was no fbi raid at biden's many homes. Again we see dishonest, anti-conservative justice.

We'll also point out that many of the liberal antifa members who burned Seattle, and took over downtown Seattle for six weeks several years ago, did not face justice. They even expelled all police from that area, burned business after business and destroyed police property. None have been prosecuted, because they are liberal, and liberal democrats can't break laws, since no laws apply to them.

So let's face the reality here; conservatives in the USA do not get fair justice, and liberal democrats are forgiven any breach of the law. We are into revolution territory here and have only a few ways out of this conundrum; the main one being a Trump victory in the next presidential election.

I guess, I'll get to work on that. I love the America promised by the US Constitution; I believe in that America, and not the bastardized, dishonest, one-sided government we now have in Washington, DC. I'm fairly sure Trump does too.

Trump believes in open, honest government, so once again, Hold My Beer!

REFLECTION 14:

Thank You for Deprogramming Me!

William N. Bender, Ph.D.

J ust when I think there may be no other topics for a Christian conservative to write about, I'm handed a giant leftist, exceptionally-woke TURD! It is like magic how frequently these woke TURDs emerge! This one came from that dear old very unimportant woman, Hillary, just this past week.

Big news for me and all Trump supporters, and really all conservatives! Hillary Clinton, the same IDIOT that labeled me and most of us as "deplorable" several years ago, has now suggested that all conservatives, all "cult followers" of President Trump—that's right all 83 million conservative Americans that voted for him-- should be "deprogrammed!" She views us all as a "cult" following a disgraced cult leader, something akin to the myopic followers of Charlie Manson or the idiots that followed Jim Jones and died because of their belief in his message. She believes we all, all 83 million of us, should be forced into some type of "deprogramming training" that would show us the error of our ways! Presumably such deprogramming would show us how horrible a person President Trump is, and why we should not support him any further. Hillary is so kind to offer, or suggest deprogramming so many Americans, isn't she? Makes one just wish to say, thanks!

While it is more than easy to poke some fun at this travesty, we do have to take this seriously. I mean this old, unimportant woman really means what she says, and after all she was, for a time, a US Senator and a serious presidential candidate. Of course, her first claim to fame was working for Barry Goldwater—a notorious conservative, many years ago. However, she was presumably "deprogrammed" at some point from such horrid conservativism, and ultimately became the flamingly woke liberal we see today. She then married a sexual predator, a serious womanizer, and a consummate, accomplished liar—poster boy of the democrats--who also served as President of the USA. During the 2016 presidential campaign, She had her staff pay a former Russian spy to invent a story about Trump colluding with Russia to suborn a presidential election in the USA. Of course, at the time she was herself, colluding with Russia to suborn a presidential election in the USA. I couldn't make this stuff up if I tried folks!

Only after an investigation began on her collusion in the lies about President Trump, did she then commit the crime of destroying evidence that was under subpoena, thus committing another federal crime. This is who wants 83 million Americans "deprogrammed!" So much for the opinions of this old, useless woman.

Still, conservatives must take note of this view, simply because such "deprogramming" is already happening. As I've mentioned previously in this Diary, many millions of Americans have had to sit through "deprogramming" sessions at their workplace on the imaginary "systematic racism" in America, where we learn that "all white people are racists" and "blacks can not be racist because they have no power." The clear untruth of these propositions is evident, once someone honestly looks at the statements. Did Obama not have power when he sat in the Oval Office? On a more scary note, doesn't kamla harris have power now? That massive collection of underused grey matter is one step away from becoming the most powerful person in the free world, and given the obvious youth of our current president, that fact should scare you to death.

Still, this deprogramming that Hillary wants to force on all conservatives, is designed to show us all that systematic racism, white privilege, and other imaginary ideas, are somehow true! According to Senator Tim Scott, all of these ideas are simply not true, but Hillary and the woke left want all Americans to agree with these foolish propositions. Thus, the "deprogramming" goes on, under the guise of "professional development" in education, medicine, industry, and many other businesses and workplaces as well.

Again, doesn't it make you want to say, "Thanks, Hillary, for helping me get the right political attitudes! Maybe one day, I can be as good a person as you and Bill!"

Again, that is sarcasm. I think it is completely un-American to force workers in any business or industry to sit through political indoctrination programs such as this, programs or in-service activities that have virtually nothing to do with their job, and are based in lies, and half-truths, even when these programs are presented as "efforts to help us all be more fair." When anyone forces workers to sit through lessons on ideas that are simply wrong, that employer should be sued for fostering a hostile work environment. I hope to see such lawsuits in the news soon, and I'm glad to note that various persons have called out their business employers for this kind of crap already.

We must no longer sit by and allow these dishonesties to grow in influence. As Christian conservatives, we must call out these attempts to "deprogram" conservatives; programs that demand agreement with woke, leftist political ideas that are untrue.

Further, while I object to, and will fight against, "deprogramming" in any form, I just can't leave this reflection here without pointing out the very real need to "deprogram" liberals and woke politicians. As our economics, our Southern border, and biden's reversal this past week on the value of "building a wall" (which he apparently now supports) indicate, the ideas of the 'woke' left are horribly wrong, and simply don't work. Here are a few realities from the news headlines today that prove this.

Our Southern Border is so broken that even biden is now building a wall, after he stated many times that building a wall won't work. Of course, he lives in a large White House, with a wall all the way around it, complete with armed guards. That wall seems to work for him.

Our economy has been broken by biden and his policies, and Americans see it every day in grocery stores. With that in mind, here's a brief guide for everyone on our future economy.

Your retirement plan hinges on having at least one successful kid!

Our schools are broken, this is clear in our government forcing LGBTQ doctrines, and other woke policies onto our teachers and ultimately our children. Do you want your child told by some woke teacher that he or she is racist simply because they are white?

Our energy sector is broken. Under Trump we were energy independent, and under biden we are destroying our own domestic energy industries, and begging our enemies to produce more oil to sell to us. How can that possibly make sense, even to a democrat?

Our cities are broken, and most have become a hellscape of woke politics in which homeless encampments, BLM, "defund the police movements" Antifa, and rampant crime skyrocket. Cities have gotten so bad that even successful businesses that make money in those cities are leaving them. Would you want to live in Chicago, downtown Seattle or San Francisco?

Biden's dream of EV cars and trucks won't work. We'll not replace gas powered vehicles any time soon, without new and improved technology, so biden's goals in this area are simply hogwash.

These are realities, and can be seen in the news daily. These realities force the question, who still supports biden and these woke ideologies? Who in the hell is that 27% of Americans that think biden and the woke liberals in Washington DC are doing great running this country? Clearly they are wrong, perhaps mentally disturbed, or brainwashed somehow. They obviously need our help. Shouldn't we begin to think about deprogramming them?

REFLECTION 15:

Israel Attacked: War In the Gaza Strip!

William N. Bender, Ph.D.

Hard to believe that the headlines on how bad things have gotten under our demented president just keep coming! I barely have time to write about one set of idiotic ideas or events, before another one presents itself. Here is today's news.

After an unprovoked and unexpected surprise attack on Israel civilians, an attack that initially killed some 250 Israeli men, women, and children in southern Israel, the government in Israel is at war. Hamas, a Palestinian organization did this rocket attack and invasion of Israeli territory, with help from others. Here is what is known today, less than two days after the horrendous attack. At this point, over 1100 persons on both sides have been killed, including many women and children, and Hamas holds over 100 hostages. Even the Japanese during WW II, as horrible as that nation was to American prisoners, didn't take hostages. This terror tactic alone shows the horrendous nature of Muslim intentions in the middle east.

Now, Israel is counter attacking portions of Israel that were taken with the Israeli Air Force, their special forces, and other assets. Israel has recaptured most of the territory in Israel that Hamas had taken in the initial attack, and is now mopping up in those areas. Israel has announced it will use just over 100,000 reserve troops and attack the Gaza Strip itself in the next 48 hours. They intend to destroy the ability of Hamas to mount further surprise attacks such as this. Because the population density in the Gaza Strip is so high (over two million people live in that short strip of land), there are likely to be many more civilian deaths on both sides.

Hamas has stated that several organizations, specifically Hezbollah, and the nation of Iran, helped coordinate the initial attack, and that's where the good old USA gets involved. Less than two months ago, our demented president paid some six billion dollars to Iran for five prisoners held in that country—yes, under biden and other presidents, our nation has paid for the release of prisoners. We do, in fact, negotiate with terrorists, and always have. Now the government of the USA has assured us all that the six billion dollars that biden released to Iran was not connected to this attack on Israel. Good to know that, if you trust this demented president and our current government. Personally, I don't. Biden and his government have declared me and all Trump supporters terrorists—and as noted before, they wish to deprogram me. I don't trust this government at all. You shouldn't either.

President biden has stated unlimited support for Israel since this attack (yes he was able to put two or three sentences together—I was pleased with that!), but other demented democrats such as AOC and other squad members including the two muslim women now serving in the US House of Representatives have taken this occasion to criticize Israel for "oppression of the population of the Gaza Strip," and thereby tried to justify this terrorist attack. Can anyone imagine a member of the Congress, on December 8, 1941 saying something like, "We'll just have to forgive the Japanese for the attack yesterday. After all our governmental policy has been horrid to Japan!" Such is the sorry state of democrats today. I should mention that in Times Square there has already been a demonstration in support of Palestine! Of course, that is in New York City, and like California, that city seems to collect idiots.

As to our government, where were they? This makes one want to ask, if the cia, the US armed forces, the defense intelligence agency, and nsa, and the fbi can consider parents at PTA meetings, all Catholics, and MAGA supporters terrorists, what do they think of real terrorists like Hamas? Have they all been spending their time watching out for horrible terrorists like me and other Christian conservatives? Have they been too busy to watch or listen in to Hamas? Now, I haven't seen these terrorist Catholics, or crazed parents at PTA meetings firing rockets into civilian living quarters. Have you? Why is our government wasting time on imaginary terrorists and ignoring real threats? What does that mean for our safety here in the USA?

Our government seems to be so concerned with the political correctness required by Wokeness, they have missed the work they could have been doing to detect this attack before it happened. Of course it takes serious time and effort to root out the imaginary white supremacy in the USA, to keep parents who disagree with LGBTQ books and instruction under watch, and make sure that all members of our armed forces use the correct pronouns! Under biden's pitifully weak presidency, these have been the major thrusts of our military and intelligence agencies. In short, we are screwed.

So how can a war in the middle east impact us? That is unknown. What is known is that one assassination of a minor member of Slavic royalty was the match that began WW I. When two dictators, Stalin and Hitler, subdivided Poland, WW II began. One event was fairly minor, while the other was a major event—still, both resulted in millions of deaths. Virtually anything can start a war, but I have every confidence that our demented president will be able to handle things, right? Sarcasm there. Have to wonder who is really running this country.

I should mention something that many suspect—that Obama still is, and has been running our government, and using old slow joe as a figurehead. Given obama's muslim background, and his hatred for all things American, his running things would make a lot of sense. He'd want to give six billion dollars to an arch enemy, as long as it was a muslim country, and an enemy of the USA. Iran clearly is both. He'd want an attack on Israel, again, because most Muslims do, and good old barry was raised muslim for almost all of his childhood. While there is no overt evidence that Obama is still running the show in our government, there are a few tantalizing facts. He is the only president who chose to remain in Washington, DC after his term ended, and many present cabinet members are routinely seen entering his home and the office he rented in DC. Are they there for a drink and a few hugs, or to get marching orders on how to help destroy America? Again, we can't say, because there is no clear evidence, but it is worth asking the question. If true, this would be one of the only things that would make today's headlines make sense.

Dr. Turley, a political commentator I do trust, has pointed out another interesting idea. It seems that Israel and a muslim country, Saudi Arabia, were about to embark on a history making move toward peace. Saudis represent the Sunni Muslims around the world, which is some 85% of all muslims. Iran is the bastion of Shia muslims. Of course, the more radical Shia would want no deal between any muslim country and Israel, and one good way to blow such a peace move out of the water is to start a war between any muslims anywhere, and Israel. The muslims in the Gaza Strip, partially ruled by Hamas, were the perfect powerkeg. Thus, war with Israel equals no peace between Israel and Saudi Arabia. Again, no hard evidence here, but an interesting idea. Look up Dr. Steve Turley on YouTube, and watch a few of his videos. I find them useful.

For me, all I can do is write, and pray. I pray for Israel. They should defend themselves just as every country should, and I'll pray for their victory and ultimately, a meaningful peace in that land. Meanwhile, this will be a bloody, hopefully short war, but it could lead to a much larger war.

Again, we can pray.

And while my head is bowed, I'll ask a blessing on this country as well. I'll ask for improved (or at least sensible, non-demented) leadership. A strong president is good for the USA and the whole world. I'll be praying for that too.

William N. Bender, Ph.D.

REFLECTION 16:

Are We Going In?

William N. Bender, Ph.D.

I had to get this and the next reflection out to folks who may be interested. The world seems to increasingly demand, reasonable, honest analysis, so here's the question: Is American about to get into a wider war in the middle east?

My last reflection highlighted the new war in the Hamas attack on Israel, and Israel was responding by bombing he Gaza Strip—the stronghold from which Hamas attacks came. Over the last few days a number of events have taken place that beg the question, is America about to enter into this war? Here are some concerning developments.

Israel has now been attacked from a second front. Another terror organization, Hezbollah, which is mainly based in southern Lebanon, just north of Israel has now fired rockets into Israel, and the Israeli Air Force has responded by bombing this region. Hezbollah is so strong, as a terror organization that it effectively runs Lebanon, and thus, we have not only Iran as a terror state in the region, but Lebanon as well. This raises the very real possibility of a two or three front war between Israel and several power players in the middle east.

We are seeing how intentionally cruel the original Hamas attackers were. Families were killed in the initial attack in various locations, often in front of each other, and one report suggested that at one Israeli settlement, 40 babies were massacred, some by beheading. There is controversy about that report, but such actions would be in keeping with Islamic terror attacks overall. One report from a body recovery team in Israel indicated that at one Jewish settlement, 80% of the recovered Jewish bodies showed signs of pre-death torture. That same source also reported that children were tied together in two different instances, and then burned alive. This is pure evil.

To make matters worse, Hamas has taken many Israeli men, women, and children hostage and is threatening to kill hostages one at a time, in retaliation for Israeli attacks. Many citizens of other countries are likewise among the hostages. While some hostages have now been rescued, there are still over 200 persons believed to be held hostage.

Slow joe initially promised American support for Israel, and America has now delivered military support. America has landed ammunition planes in Israel. Also the Gerald R. Ford Carrier Group steamed toward Israel and is now anchored offshore. Another American carrier group is likewise heading for that country. Biden visited Israel on day 10 of this conflict, and said he stands with Israel, but he also announced that the US would be providing 100 million (my tax dollars, and yours), to humanitarian aid for Palestinians in the Gaza strip and West Bank. This puts significant American military assets directly into the war zone, but also gives 100 million dollars indirectly to terrorists, who are still in control of the Strip and the West Bank. Only an idiot would do that, and this is what must be expected from a demented president.

A small number of US politicians –all progressive, woke, democrats of course, the one's that hate America as well as Israel—have refused to condemn the Hamas attacks, and asked all sides to deescalate. It seems rather one sided to request de-escalation right after a horrendous attack has been made, but what can one expect of democrats?

Various American cities and cities around the world have seen demonstrations in support of Hamas and the Palestinians. Several members of the Squad of progressive democrats were present at those demonstrations. What can one expect of such people?

To date, we know that over 2000 Israeli citizens and a similar number of people in Gaza have died, along with 25 Americans in this war.

As I mentioned in a previous reflection, Saudi Arabia was making a serious effort toward normalization with Israel. That effort is now on hold for a time. In that sense, this meaningless war, this slaughter of innocents, makes sense in the mind of Hamas leaders, leaders in Iran, and elsewhere who are committed to ending the state of Israel.

More horrid news. Slow Joe said that Americans are among those held hostage by Hamas. One has to ask, does biden plan to give six billion to Hamas, as he did to Iran, to purchase these hostages too? He has, as noted above, already given money to folks in Gaza for "humanitarian aid" but with Hamas as the only real power there, he is once again, giving money to terrorists. One can only hope not, but we have to ask, how much does biden, and ultimately Obama, really hate Israel? I suspect that Obama is really running the country at this point. I mean, lets face facts; Joe biden cannot put together a coherent sentence, so someone has to be pulling strings in D.C.. There. I said it.

Some things are better left unsaid. I usually realize that right after I say them.

These facts are horrible, and may suggest that a much wider war is coming in this region. American military assets are already in the area. Other bad actors are getting more involved by day 10, as I update this reflection. Iran has announced war with Israel, should Israel actually invade the Gaza Strip, and North Korean weapons are being used by Hamas. Many bombing raids have taken place in Gaza, and some against Hezbollah in Southern Lebanon, to the north of Israel. Also, Turkey has expressed support for Israel, and they are supposedly our ally; they are a member of NATO, but they are also a muslim country. In almost every way, this looks like a much wider war is coming.

There is however one ray of hope. We have to note that America has done a good job of avoiding directly entering any of the recent wars in the middle east. We have supported Israel, and I hope we continue to do, but we have not had boots on the ground, or American airmen in the air fighting at all. I can only hope that this continues, but with the war seeming to expand daily, and America sending the types of support that we are sending, one has to wonder, are we going into Israel, the Gaza Strip, Lebanon, or elsewhere in the middle east.

Again, I must pray. I hope you do too. I'll pray for peace in the middle east ultimately, but prior to that I'll pray for Israeli success in putting an end to Hamas power, ending Hezbollah influence in Lebanon, and a serious reconning with Iran. If we truly want peace in this region, the evil players who practice hatred as a way of life, and want only war must be driven from power, as we once did to Hitler.

It is not an exaggeration to say that Hamas and these other bad actors are as evil as Hitler was. Those burned bodies of children provide all the evidence any sane person would need, as did the ovens in the WW II concentration camps. The evidence of evil here is clear. I hope Israel will bring these evil power players to a just end.

William N. Bender, Ph.D.

REFLECTION 17:

They Drink the Kool-aid! Explaining a Liberal

William N. Bender, Ph.D.

I just watched a documentary on the mass suicide of the followers of Jim Jones, on November 18, 1978. Jones had started a Christian church in San Francisco, but left the United States to go into the jungle in Guyana and build a "paradise" where there was "social justice for all." According to Jones' own son, his father was a power-hungry, charismatic preacher, who had been crazy even before the mass murder-suicide. Still, with the press about to expose Jones' sexual exploits and emotional abuse of his followers, he convinced 908 apparently sane people to commit suicide. They "drank the Kool-aid" knowing the drink was laced with poison, because Jones—a known socio-path--told them to do it. It is difficult to imagine what types of mental pressures were placed on those people, and while some were, apparently forced-fed the drink, most took that drink willingly. They were led to their death by a man who, himself, was so captured by drugs he was losing control of his own mental state anyway, and was sure that everyone in America was out to get him. Because he was trusted by his followers, they willingly died at his order.

I could likewise write a paragraph here about the deaths of 76 persons in Waco, Texas, where another power-crazed madman, David Koresh, pretended to preach the Gospel of Jesus, all the while empowering himself, not Jesus and the Christian message. Like Jones he was power hungry, committed sexual abuse of children, and placed intense psychological pressures on his followers, and like Jones he managed to convince a number of followers to resist US law. On April 19, 1993, the feds raided the Branch Davidian compound, looking for firearms. Shots were fired and fire broke out in the buildings. That botched fbi siege led to the death of 76 people. Like Jones' followers, those Branch Davidians apparently, drank the Kool-aid; they chose to follow a madman to their own death.

Don't Drink the Kool-aid!

That phrase "don't drink the Kool-aid" actually originated with the Jonestown event in 1978, and while there are similarities in the events above, there are significant differences too. Still, one has to wonder, why do reasonable, sane people drink the Kool-aid when a madman says to do so? Are some people so weak of will that they can be led to kill themselves simply by an order from a charismatic lunatic?

Of course, most of you have figured where I'm going with this—just consider the title above. I want to know how reasonably sane people become liberals. How can someone in today's world who actually has a brain become, or remain, a liberal democrat? Can they not see the harsh reality that our country was on the right track under President Trump, and has been going wrong since the day biden took office? We have China threatening war, a real war in Israel that threatens to broaden into a regional conflict, gas prices through the roof, and grocery prices are even worse. Our southern border is a disaster, so much so that even liberal democratic mayors are complaining about those "open border" democratic policies, and one or two liberal democrats have even chosen to become republican!

How bad does it have to be before liberals realize that their policies are killing us all? Biden's poll number are, admittedly in the toilet, with something like 70% of Americans saying the country is heading in the wrong direction. Still, I want to know who the other guys are? Who are that 27% of Americans that think biden is doing just dandy? Are they all

103

crazy, or did someone drink the Kool-aid here? These folks are as demented as biden himself, but they talked themselves into believing in non-reality instead of reality. They drank the Kool-aid!

When I think of such folks, I sincerely want people to understand the effort I put in to not being a serial killer.

Maybe I'll never understand that, but as the examples of extremism above show, reasonably sane people can be taught to agree with virtually anything, when it is presented in the right way, by one or more charismatic figures. Democrats can produce charismatic leaders—generally leaders who fail, but charismatic none the less. I'd suggest both Bill Clinton and Obama fall into that camp—charismatic leaders with really bad policies. Don't forget that Obama's policies actually helped Iran maintain a nuclear program, and Hillary Clinton sold uranium to that evil country, so if we see a dirty bomb some time this week go off in Israel or America, we know who to thank!

Still, does this explain liberalism, and the apparent, obvious insanity one has to practice to actually be a liberal? Here are some of their other insane beliefs.

Walls on borders don't work (The reality: they do work, so much so that all rich liberals live in walled-in homes or compounds. Even the White House in DC has a wall around it).

Gas engines are destroying the planet (the reality: fossil fuels have provided the highest standard of living ever seen on the planet, and it could not have happened without these fuels).

Guns should be outlawed to protect citizens from gun violence (the reality: guns owned by citizens, actually lead to reduced crime, and the science shows that. The only thing that really stops a bad guy with a gun, is a good guy with a gun!).

Defunding the police while funding social workers to resolve domestic disputes will reduce deaths at the hands of cops (the reality: domestic disputes are one of the most dangerous situations cops find themselves in. Most of the cities that have defunded police have seen a rather drastic increase in all crime).

Israel should end the war against Gaza! (the reality: ending a war against evil tyrants is appeasement; It is like giving Hitler total control over Europe, forever. It would be insane for Israel to cease fire now, but liberals are calling for exactly that! How dumb can they be?).

This list could go on and on, but even if we listed all liberal insanities, we still would not be closer to understanding how a liberal can actually believe the crap they believe! For example, as biden not to mention more and more Hollywood personalities, tell everyone that climate change is the single biggest threat in the world today, the weak minded might actually begin to believe that. Is that how a liberal can be a liberal? Is that how someone can bring themselves to vote for democrats and democratic policies like those above? Apparently, a charismatic leader is all that is needed to get people to believe anything. I've suggested as much in this Diary previously when I pointed out that Hitler, another charismatic leader, was able to convince one of the most highly educated populations on earth to do the most horrible things to their fellowman. In short, people can be convinced to believe anything in the right circumstances.

Research on the Garden of Eden story has shown that men will gladly eat any fruit given them by a naked woman.

In my lifetime, for example, there has been serious debate about the direction of temperature change in our world's climate. Is the world heating up or cooling down? That was still an open question in the 1970s when I went to college. Moreover, if the climate is indeed changing, does that change really result from the activities of man, or is it a cycle of nature? These are unanswered questions and sane people will not want to pretend that the issue of "Climate change" is the most serious issue confronting America right now, as biden continues to insist. Still, there are liberals out there that believe it—they drank the Kool-aid.

Today we know that the North Pole is still frozen (climate changers several years ago stated that it would be free of ice by 2014—wrong again). We also know that the polar bear population is growing like crazy (They were supposed to be extinct by now. Climate changers were wrong again). Finally, I remember being told in college that, while the issue was availability of oil in 1973, that by the time I retired, it would be "Water." Yes, water was supposed to be a scarce commodity by now, according to early climate change beliefs—wrong again. How can anyone, anyone who is honest, be so consistently wrong and yet maintain their beliefs in the "danger" of climate change? Clearly these woke liberals drank some high powered Kool-aid! Wonder what drugs were in that stuff?

In the 60s I took LSD to make the world look weird. Now it is weird, and I take Prozac to make it look normal.

Now we might be tempted to just leave this discussion here; liberals drank from the liberal Kool-aid fountain, and so they either are dumb enough to believe the types of things above, or they choose to believe it. So what? If that was all there was to it, then the issue of how they can believe the stuff they believe would not be really important, and I wouldn't put it here in the diary. I mean, dumb animals don't worry me all that much.

Still, the problem with liberals is that their beliefs motivate them to attack you and me—we conservative deplorables and all the other folks that actually love and respect America. The hatred and destruction that these self-righteous liberals intentionally cause, hurts our country and many of us individually. These woke liberals are so driven by their desperate illusions that they will villainize anyone who disagrees with them. They cancel people; they make false, misleading accusations to silence people. They will even feel justified, righteous somehow, in their beliefs, so much so that they will attempt to destroy all who disagree. That is what wokeism is all about—silencing any who disagree with liberal perspectives. As the recent pro-Hamas protests have shown, liberal democrats believe in their own lies (see those above) so much that they are willing to accept and seemingly forgive torturing and killing innocent children simply because they are Jewish. It is hard to imagine this level of hatred.

So again, how can Christians respond? While turning the other cheek is a clear guideline, I'm not sure Jesus meant that Christians should willingly line their children up and pour on the gasoline to help Hamas burn them alive. We, as Christians, can resist non-violently by speaking out against the evil of Hamas, and the evils of the democratic woke liberals who support them. I'd put all democrats in that basket, since, even if they didn't express support for Hamas, they have expressed support for biden's open border, the trans-gender movement, CRT, Black Lives Matter and other hate filled groups. That single failed policy of the open border alone could put Hamas agents anywhere in America today, along with their evil intentions, and arms similar to what we've seen used against Israel.

Once again, I just want to shout out, Thank you Mr. Biden!

Ok, sarcasm again. Still, enough liberals in American have, apparently drunk the Kool-aid. We cannot ignore this, because this is so dangerous to us all, and to the America that we love. We must begin to oppose these woke liberals with our words, our money, our time and our votes, or we will be destroyed—as dead as the bodies of those burned children that Hamas has left for all the world to see. Further, unless we oppose these evils we will not have any free country left. That was the case in 1941, and it is the case now.

May God protect and defend Israel, against all evil attacks. May God likewise protect America, from the evils like Hamas. Finally, may God open the eyes of those woke democrats so that they ultimately see, in the burned bodies of the children in Israel, how their own policies are leading to destruction of the greatest bastion of freedom in the history of the world, the American Constitutional government. May we, once and for all, educate all liberals to look at reality; to not drink the liberal Kool-aid, or in the end, they will end up just as dead as those followers of Jim Jones so many years ago.

REFLECTION 18:

America Fires First US Shots in Israeli War

*A*s I write this today (October 20, 2023), it was announced that America had fired the first shot in the growing conflict in Israel. Apparently, several terrorist organizations have joined the war against Israel, and one fired missiles from the country of Yemen toward Israel. An American destroyer, the USS Carney, stationed in the Red Sea fired on 3 airborne missiles and several drones and destroyed them all. The Pentagon spokesperson said that this defensive action was the type of action the US would take to protect US interests and US allies in that region.

Raptor News also reported that missiles were fired on several off-shore oil rigs belonging to Israel in the Mediterranean Sea, and that Israel defense forces destroyed those missiles. This is a concern because the United States has two aircraft carriers located near those oil rigs, and while the targets of those missiles appeared to be the oil rigs themselves, the US carriers and the other ships in the carrier battle groups were on location nearby. Of course, carriers and battle groups carry extensive self-defense capabilities, and realistically there was virtually no possibility that any US ships would have been hit by only 3 missiles. Had the IDF not taken down those missiles, US defenses would have done so. Still, this attack may indicate something of an escalation of the role of America in this proxy war.

Also, the attack brings into focus the sheer stupidity of these terrorist organizations. Did they really think they could fire 3 missiles anywhere near

American warships and actually hit anything? Have they not noticed that America is a bit more prepared than in those heady days, when a ski-boat put a hole in the USS Cole?

Ignorance can be educated, crazy can be medicated, but there's no cure for stupid.

While it is easy to poke fun at stupidity of these guys, we do have to take serious note of the intensity of hatred this enemy has for Israel and the United States. During my lifetime, American forces have been attacked a number of times, and it rarely ends well for the attackers. However, those attackers know that and are nevertheless so motivated with hatred that they will attack us anyway. The example of 9/11/01 comes to mind, when 19 hate filled men decided to conduct an attack on American soil, and drove four aircraft into 3 buildings and one cornfield. All of the buildings were loaded with people, and over 3000 Americans died. They hit the cornfield, because some brave Americans on one aircraft fought back, and that plane nose-dived killing only those on board, including those brave Americans. Authorities suspect that plane was headed for the White House. Still, did those 19 guys really think they could accomplish anything of meaning? Once again, sheer hatred, whether of Israel or America, seems to be simply mindless.

How can these people hate so much that they act so stupidly? Cleary, in the middle east hatred is taught to Islamic children from a very young age, and over several generations such hatred can be quite motivational. Such hatred is the exact opposite of the love Jesus showed, to virtually everyone he met. Jesus even recommended loving one's enemies, and he showed how to do that as he hung from a cross, and prayed for those who were torturing and killing him. That is merely one aspect of the amazing story of Jesus. In many ways, such overwhelming love is the exact opposite of muslim beliefs.

Still, teaching such hatred to one's children as many muslims do makes no sense in the long run—it merely condemns those children to a very unpleasant life, a hate filled life.

It is now 10/22/23, and Israel has not yet invaded the Gaza Strip. They have not announced why they are on hold (probably conducting secret negotiations, and secret raids to locate and liberate hostages). The bombing runs over Gaza continue.

The war in northern Israel and lower Lebanon is growing, and Israel continues to pound Hezbollah locations on that northern front. Because Hezbollah is merely a puppet of Iran, the Iranian government has cautioned Israel not to invade the Gaza Strip. In turn Israel had announced that it might raid targets in Iran, making this an even wider war.

With Israel holding the strongest war machine in the entire region, by far, one has to wonder at the hatred-motivated stupidity of Iran. They could hurt Israel, yes, but if outright war between those two came, Iran could never win. It would be ultimate suicide for Iran to go to war with Israel, but those muslims really do hate that much. Again, hatred is simply stupid. For anyone with a brain, teaching hatred is simply, maddeningly, inexplicable. It makes my brain hurt.

Now I realize that it is God's business to judge, and I know that one day he will judge us all. And yes, I know that I'll need forgiveness too, probably a bit more than most, and I do understand that all sin, large or small, holds us away from God's presence. Still, is it small, or even petty of me to hope he judges those most harshly who teach hatred to their children, generation after generation? Am I wrong to hope that harsh, Old-Testament justice will soon fall on those who burn innocent children alive? God's wrath appeared as burning sulfur raining down from Heaven, when he chose to destroy Sodom and Gomorrah. Is it wrong to wish for a mushroom cloud or two over Iran and Hezbollah locations in southern Lebanon? It's hard to love any enemies, as Jesus instructed, but it is particularly hard to love such cruel enemies!

Patience is what you need when there are simply too many witnesses.

Again, tonight, I'll be praying that America not go to war. I'll be praying for Israel, that they can win, and perhaps eliminate the hatred of Hamas and Hezbollah for all time. Perhaps then, with God's help, a lasting peace can be established in that region.

Let's all pray that we live to see a day of "Peace on Earth, good will to all men." We need Jesus; I need Jesus, and his love now, more than ever, and I when I see this level of intentional cruelty, I need it much more than most.

William N. Bender, Ph.D.

REFLECTION 19:

The Grown Ups are Back in Charge!

William N. Bender, Ph.D.

*A*s we witness the unfolding of not one, but two different wars, both of which America is intimately involved with, one has to consider how much better things are under biden than they were under President Trump. As we can see, when biden took office, it became very clear that the grown-ups were back in charge.

Wify tells me often I have to watch out for my sarcasm but this world is so very crazy that I cannot help myself sometimes, so please forgive me for that paragraph above.

Many of you guys will remember that the mainstream media, that ever honest bastion of truth and justice (sorry, there I go again), used the same talking point when biden took the white house a few years ago. It was so very obvious at the time that Fox News ran a segment in which they showed ten or twelve talking-heads from other networks and news outlets saying the same talking point. Yep, you guessed it:

The Grown-ups are back in charge!

Once you see ten or more supposedly independent news commentators, from various networks using the same phrase it becomes obvious that those folks were coached to use that language; it was a talking point that some democratic staffer made up, and then fed to the mainstream news outlets. With biden in the White House, "the grown-ups were back in charge!" And like the brainless talking heads they are, the mainstream news media people regurgitated the same line, repeatedly. That compilation of news commentators saying the same thing was hilarious.

And just who are these grown-ups? They have to be the democrats in the White House, and the Senate, and US House of Representatives. This means biden and harris (twiddle de dumb and twiddle de de) have to be in the group. Neither of them can put a coherent sentence together, and they are the two most powerful people in our nation! That is really scary when you think about it.

Pelosi, dear old Nancy, would have to be included. She led the US House of Representatives until 2020, so of course she'd be included here. While Republicans took control of the House in 2020, Nancy is still around, as aging leader of the old-folks club that is the democratic leadership. Of course, the Senate and White House are still in control of the democrats, the grown-ups! Schummer—that Jewish prince—leads the democrats in the senate and one has to wonder how the man lives with himself. I mean, democrats absolutely hate Israel (the squad in particular), and this guy is Jewish, so how does this guy sleep at night? Perhaps a simple review of legal issues for some in this group will help clarify things.

Cocaine was found in biden's house. Nothing happened. A dead body was found at obama's house. Nothing happened. A male prostitute was found at pelosi's house. Nothing happened. A few out of date papers were found in Florida, so the fbi raided Trump's house. One has to wonder about that!

Now that we know who those "grown-ups" are, we might want to consider their amazing accomplishments to date! The headlines today simply beg for a review of how well the "grown-ups" are doing. Now let me think.

Regular gas costs 2.19 a gallon here in Georgia on the day biden took office (Yes, I actually looked the day biden took office!). Because slow *joe immediately began his war on American energy, killing the Keystone Pipeline, and restricting new oil leases, the gas price went to well over $3 in less than six months. Then it went higher. While it has come back down a bit recently, nobody has seen a price of 2.19 again. Now slow joe is coming for almost all gas powered kitchen appliances—since they represent such a serious threat to us all!*

Groceries are up so much that people make jokes about investing in "eggs!" I've seen estimates of 20% to 40% increases in grocery prices. Personally, (wify and I own some rental houses, as investments) I've seen tenants with large families who cannot feed them and pay the rent at the same time. Clearly the grown-ups must be doing a great job!

I do have to mention the southern and northern border. These borders are another disaster created by these grown-ups. How many Hamas terrorists have come into America and are hiding here in plain sight? Now I'm not talking about the woke, progressive democrats in the US House—those terrorists squad members sympathizing with Hamas. We at least know who they are. I'm talking about the uncounted scores, or hundreds or thousands of terrorists crossing our borders (both north and south) monthly. In 2023, there has been 2,475,000 encounters with folks coming in illegally, according to Fox News, and 172 of those were on the terror watch list. In contrast, in 2019 with Trump in charge, we found 3 persons on the terror watch list. That is a hefty increase under slow joe, and this begs the question, how many have we not caught? We're still doing "catch and release" in Texas, Arizona, California, and elsewhere, so nobody really knows if Hamas now has 25 or 100, or 2,000 hate-filled, trained, armed operatives in the US. Maybe that number is 10,000! Who knows? Once again, the grown-ups are back in charge!

But wait! Theres More!

The stuff above, that's all on the domestic front. As we consider how well the grown-ups in the biden administration are doing, we have to get to the fun stuff in foreign policy. I mean, the domestic stuff might starve us all to death over time, but biden level stupidity in foreign policy could flat-out kill us all, so here goes.

Just this week, the infamous "five eyes" group (the heads of five major intelligence agencies, including the USA) released a warning about China. China is gearing up for a major war with the USA, and seems to be partnering with Russia, and North Korea, and Iran. What fun those evil powers could bring into the world! I wonder if that would have happened under Trump (we know that it did not), or did this coalition arise, and perhaps even require an amazingly weak, and ineffectual leader in the White House? I have to think anyone who voted for biden can be thanked for our problems now. Well, anyway, it's good to know that the grown-ups are back in charge!

Of course, several leaders of the American Military have warned of a coming war with China. About a year ago, one Senior General actually predicted such a war by 2025. I wonder if anyone in the White House heard him. I wonder if anyone in the White House cares? Still, take comfort, after all the grown-ups are back in charge!

This brings us to the wars. Under slow joe and the grown-ups, Russia decided to steal the Ukraine back from the Ukrainians. I mean, after all, Russia is still allowed to steal property, while all other nations around the world are criticized for being "colonizers" during recent centuries. America, in contrast conquers lands and then sets up democracies (German and Japan, and South Korea as recent examples). Still, Russia is allowed to simply steal land, and is given a pass by the mainstream media. Russia took lands in Chechnya when Obama was president, and under biden Russia has tried to steal the Ukraine. Weak, woke democrats seem to be in the process of making Russia bigger, if not stronger.

It is interesting to note that under President Trump, Russia didn't grab any land at all. I wonder why? Could it be that Trump was a strong President? Perhaps we should share that insight with democrats. Are they honest enough to see that reality? Just kidding—they aren't.

115

Now, I've commented on the war in Israel above—it is ongoing and growing into a regional conflict. Under obama and biden billions of dollars were given to Iran, and that nation created and funds Hamas, so the Israeli War of 2023 was really a war with Iran. The war was planned in Iran, and funded by Iran, using funds given to that country by the democratic "grown-ups!" Just this past week, biden gave my tax dollars to Hamas. In fact, we just gave 100 million tax dollars to "humanitarian" aid for people in Gaza. However, the only real political power in Gaza is, you guessed it; Hamas. I wonder if those dollars—my money—will actually go for humanitarian aid, or did slow joe just give our enemies 100 million? In Gaza, Hamas runs everything anyway. We simply gave that help to them. Doesn't it make you proud to be an American?

Well, time for the sarcasm to end I guess. Truthfully, I'm not proud of this country any more. As I've said before in this Diary, this is not the country my Dad fought for during WW II. This is not what America has been traditionally, nor what it can be.

Still, the record seems clear. With these democratic, woke, grown-ups in charge, our nation is failing by every single measure imaginable—both in foreign policy and domestically. All honest Americans have to at least, admit that! If this is how the democratic grown-ups do, then we need President Trump, or someone with his strength of character—back in the White House.

I still wonder how those folks feel who actually voted for biden in 2020. Who are the 27% of Americans that, according to recent polls, still think he's doing a good job? As I said before, they drank some powerful Kool-aid. And I have to say, if this is how grown-ups run this country, we definitely need another option!

Again, I pray for Israel, and America. Hope you do too. And I pray we can get rid of these woke, progressive, grown-ups in DC soon, while there is still a country here to save.

Postscript: On October 25, 2023, Raptor News announced that Israeli forces had entered Gaza in response to cross border attacks by Hamas. While there has been no announcement of the beginning of the anticipated Israeli offensive in Gaza by the Israeli government, this is the first time that IDF forces have entered Gaza directly. Also according to Fox News today, the US Dept. of Defense announced that US forces in the middle east have now been directly attacked by drones 14 times in the last 16 days (since the beginning of the war in Israel and Gaza), with no loss of life. This might be the beginning of the giant Israeli offensive, and thus, this could trigger a war between Israel and Iran, or a wider war.

REFLECTION 20:

A Mass Shooting in Maine

William N. Bender, Ph.D.

*L*ike most of America, I woke up to the headlines today that a mass shooter in Maine had killed at least 16 people. Some other reports, including Fox News suggested 22 persons were killed, and many more wounded, in a bar and bowling alley. The white male shooter had been admitted this past summer to a mental health facility, and was released after only two weeks. He was apparently in the US Army Reserve, and thus knew weapons and shooting procedures, and some video shows that he used a semi-automatic rifle. He is still at large, as I write this on the morning of 10/26/23.

Can't wait to see how woke democrats respond to this shooting, but here are a few possibilities.

Up in Maine, they should have defunded the police sooner!

Well, maybe the liberals are smart enough to avoid that one. They probably won't make that exact point, so I guess we are in for their only other argument; yep, you guessed it another round of meaningless arguments about assault weapons bans, and other gun control ideas that will have absolutely zero impact on mass shootings. If these things were effective, then mass shootings would not occur in gun regulated states such as California,

Colorado, or New York. If gun control worked, then Chicago and Los Angeles should be virtually free of gun violence! Of course, the opposite is true—Chicago is one of the deadliest cities in the nation for gun violence, because innocent persons living there are not allowed to protect themselves using legal firearms. So here's a basic, politically-incorrect truth:

You are your own first responder. You better be prepared!

I can report that on Fox News this morning I saw Newt Gingrich make the point that we in American need to consider "new ways to respond to mass shootings," and while he stopped short of making the exact point above, his arguments were headed in that direction. He made the point that law enforcement comes in "after the massacre." He also pointed out that the recent attacks on civilians in Israel may have been less dramatic, had many more citizens been armed.

Of course, Israel is a heavily armed nation, and there was resistance to the early attacks by Hamas three weeks ago. Still, more resistance could have made some difference, but in Israel, as here in America, there are persons who do not believe in taking up arms to protect oneself. I cannot understand that view, but many persons believe that citizens should not be armed.

Imagine if a wolf realized that his descendant would be a pug. That's how your granddad feels when he sees your man bun.

What can be proven is that an armed population results in less crime. Researcher John Lott has documented that phenomenon in research studies for decades now. His argument is simple; more guns in the hands of citizens leads to less crime, and he has consistently presented research to prove that point. As one might expect, his statistics, and his overall research has been challenged by many politically woke researchers, and ultimately this body of research is largely ignored by the "gun control" crowd. Like most woke, liberal idiots, if they don't like facts they simply ignore them. I cannot help but believe that Conservatives are much more honest—we actually look at and consider the facts before we make a decision. In short,

Liberals are, quite literally, too stupid to insult.

Conservative conspiracy theorists are not like woke liberal scientists. Most of our theories are proven true.

So for all of us, I guess the question is, do we wish to be unprotected against a mentally ill shooter, or a mugger, or a thief, or gang members wishing to steal our car, our money, or our lives? Do we trust police response times, and simply wait to die when faced with a lone crazed gunman? Do we really want to test out the "response time" of the local police in these cases, or do we want to be prepared to shoot back? Personally, my decision is clear.

I choose to be my own first responder.

Perhaps Dylan Thomas said it best. Speaking in an entirely different context, he simply says:

Do not go gentle into that good night; Rage, rage against the dying of the light.

FYI: Should I ever have to act as my own first responder, my rage will travel at 830 to 1000 FPS, the muzzle velocity of my .45. Have a nice day.

William N. Bender, Ph.D.

Today, as I send out this set of Reflections, it is Friday, 10/27/23. The US has announced that since the war in Israel began, US forces in the middle east have been attacked 20 times. Also the US is strengthening its security forces on bases in the entire area, by sending 900 additional troops to the region. Finally, Israel has now ventured again into Gaza in limited fashion, and some reports indicate that a full-on invasion by Israeli forces may be only 48 hours away, as their aircraft continue to pound targets in Gaza and southern Lebanon. Again, this looks like small stepping stones into a war for the USA. I hope all who read this will pray.

REFLECTION 21:

Thoughts on the Lusitania

Who among us bothers to remember the Lusitania? Well history majors like me for one. Those who study history, tend to respect the lessons of history, perhaps a bit more than others. So, for all of you non-history buffs, here's the scoop. The Lusitania was a British Ocean liner that was torpedoed and sunk by a German U-Boat during WW I (May 7, 1915, to be exact). It was one of the first non-combatant ships in world history ever destroyed by an enemy navy. It was sunk in British waters near Ireland, and Britian and Germany were at war. America was not fighting in WW I at that time, having chosen to remain neutral and let European nations determine the fate of European nations. So, no big deal, right?

Wrong. First of all that ship was not a combat ship—it carried paying civilians, and no weapons, officially. Now Germany had announced unrestricted warfare against all British shipping, and prior to leaving America, all the passengers were warned that they would be cruising into a war zone in a British ship. Still, no one, at the time thought Germany would actually attack a passenger liner. Germany was, after all, a civilized nation, and a European nation; a nation that was trusted to abide by general guidelines and principles against unrestricted warfare against civilians.

That "trust" of German actions, even during war is probably why some bone-head decided to load the ship as they did. The truth is the ship was *carrying some munitions for the British War effort: Over 4 million rounds of rifle cartridges, and 5,000 artillery shell casings, along with more than 3,000 percussion artillery fuses. In some sense Germany was right, in that this passenger liner, while not an armed warship (and thus defenseless), did carry arms to be used against Germany.*

However, the biggest problem occurred with the passenger list. Of the 1962 persons on board, only 761 survived. Further, one hundred and twenty-eight Americans died in that "cowardly" attack that day. British news "raised awareness" of the cruelty of sinking an unarmed passenger ship, while denying that the ship was carrying any munitions at all. America became outraged, and while historians differ, most conclude that this sinking led to America's entry into WW I in 1916, on the side of the British. Back then, America took seriously the need to protect American lives anywhere on the globe, and our nation went to war to do so. It also pays to remember that we entered the Spanish American War when the US Battleship Maine was attacked in Havana, and after 9/11 America went to war against terror. Back then we believed that America should protect Americans.

The clocks go back this weekend! I'm setting mine back to 1916, when this country had some balls, and chicks didn't!

I'll just mention, for all those woke democrats out there, that under Trump the entire middle east was quiet for years. Further Iran was heavily sanctioned and virtually bankrupt, and thus unable to fund wars by Hamas and others. We had no wars at all under a strong leader like Trump. With Trump in the White House, we tied up Iran's money, and told them to behave—they did. That is what a strong leader can do. That is what Trump did.

I came from a generation where 'just keep talking' meant you better shut up!

Now we'll just fast forward to today. We have, in slow joe, the weakest president in recent history, a man whose mind is virtually gone, and our nation (along with the rest of the world) suffers. Is any democrat today actually proud that they voted for biden? We now know (It was stated blatantly this morning on Fox News), that Americans were beheaded by Hamas; Americans were raped by Hamas, and Americans were intentionally killed right along with Israelis and civilians from many other nations, by Hamas in the attack some weeks ago. Also, it is freely admitted by all responsible news agencies that Hamas is funded mainly by Iran—yes the same Iran that Obama gave a nuclear weapons deal to, and that biden provided six billion dollars to, along with millions of dollars in smaller, less publicized ways. That six billion is still sitting in banks in Qatar and has not been given to Iran yet, but slow joe has chosen not to re-freeze those funds. Why???????

So here's were we are under slow joe. We are so stupid (that is our foreign policy is so stupid) that our tax dollars have provided the weapons, the funding, and the ability for Hamas and Hezbollah to kill not only Israelis, but Americans as well. In the video I saw today, Larry Kudlow asked the same question I do here; how stupid can we, as a nation, be? Why should we continue to fund our own enemies, WHILE THEY RAPE, BEHEAD, AND KILL AMERICANS?

This period of history will be known as the dumb ages!

My paycheck is taxed nearly in half, and then I pay taxes on everything I buy, all so woke democrats can send my money to people here who don't work or pay any taxes, or the send billions of dollars to other countries to solve their problems while America inches closer to the cliff! We now pay our enemies to kill Americans! WHY?

Now as a historian, and in order to be fair, I have to remember that during WW II, our nation sent billions of dollars to Germany and Japan, for humanitarian reasons, and some of those funds, no doubt, helped build the gas chambers used to exterminate Jews and others that Germany considered deplorable. Right?

Wrong! Dead Wrong! Not a cent of American tax dollars was handed to our enemies during that war or WW I either. We did fund the rebuilding of those nations after the war; that is what reasonable humanitarian aid looks like. Further, we didn't give funds to the North Koreans' during the Korean War either. Back then, America had strong leadership. Today we don't. As a result, the world is witnessing two wars, and America may be sucked into one in the Middle East. I'll leave this today, with the same thought I have when I buy gas or groceries;

Thank you Mr. biden! You did that!

REFLECTION 22:

Crooked Elections: Obama and Biden

William N. Bender, Ph.D

Today, November 1, 2023, Republican Congressman Jim Jordan announced that his congressional committee had discovered that both the Obama and Biden administrations had the department of injustice spy on Congressional staffers and possibly Congressmen illegally, by demanding communications records of their emails, phone records, and social media posts from Google, and possibly Verizon, Apple, and other big tech carriers. This is an impeachable offense, and if proven, might document yet another set of lies and illegalities of slow joe. At this point, one has to ask, where does the illegality of this president end? Who supports this guy? Don't you just want to thank those hard-core woke democrats for this nonsense?

I know I don't have to be sarcastic, but the world has given me so much to work with, and I would hate to be wasteful!

The good news is now that we have a Speaker of the House, various committees can get back to the investigation of the biden crime family. Representative Comer has indicated just in the last two days, that his committee has found hard evidence of payments directly to slow joe from China. This is looking more and more like bribery of the guy who is the current, though demented, leader of the free world. We are in a dangerous situation here, with two wars breaking out, and Americans have already died (as hostages) and American bases are attacked daily. How I wish we had a strong president, with all his mental faculties!

Is it an accident that "take out" can mean food, dating, or murder? Just a question!

As to what other illegalities the democrats are pulling these days, we have, for the first time in recent memory, a judicial decision overturning a crooked election—an election that turned in favor of course, of the democratic candidate. In early November, 2023, a Judge in CT overturned a local election for Mayor in Bridgeport, CT, stating that the evidence of fraud in favor of the democrat was "shocking." In that election, there were multiple instances of video footage evidence of people (all of whom were democrats and some were city employees and/or elected officials themselves) stuffing scores of ballots into ballot boxes, and some 900 absentee ballots that could not be accounted for, swung the election for the democrat (what a surprise that is--NOT!). An estimated 37% of the mail in ballots were questionable. There were also other irregularities.

We should also note that the mayor that was elected in this crooked election was earlier convicted of federal corruption-related charges and had spend 7 years in prison, according to a video story from the Epoch Times and the New York Times. In short, this particular democrat has the moral compass of slow Joe, bill and Hillary, along with other stellar democrats. I've often wondered who votes for these guys. It seems the answer may be "no one!" These guys just stuff imaginary ballots into boxes to win.

At this point, being a history buff, I have to recall the widely accepted suggestion (Never proven) that democrat John Kennedy (another bastion of moral rigor) was elected president, based on votes from dead people. The names of the dead in Chicago were copied from grave markers by members of the Mafia, who then used those names on absentee ballots, and all of those ballots were cast for democrats. Back then Chicago was run by the Daily democratic machine, and that city controlled the state of Illinois. It is a historic fact that Illinois turned that election way back in 1960 to Kennedy.

Not sure about an inner child, but I have an inner Murderer that surfaces every now and then, and he is pissed.

But back to today. The judge in CT found overwhelming evidence for a crooked election, based on many of the same types of tactics that create election fraud that many conservatives suspect helped "steal" the recent presidential election from President Trump in 2020. I've commented on that presidential election previously in this Diary. I do not know about ballot stuffing or voting machines that changed votes, as some have alleged during the presidential election in 2020, but I do know that a wide variety of news agencies have reported that the "facebook" funded foundation money went to the supposedly non-partisan effort to "get out the vote." However, those funds were almost exclusively spent in democratic districts; that is a partisan effort and non-profit funds cannot be used for partisan politics. Those millions and millions of dollars helped swing both Wisconsin and Georgia to slow joe, and using those funds in a way that favors either political party is illegal. I personally run and 501 C 3 Foundation, and I am aware of the regulations that prevent any funds in that foundation from being used for partisan politics.

So, the ray of hope here, is that in at least one local election, voter fraud has now been demonstrated. That election was overturned by the judge and a new election was ordered. Will the democrats use the same illegal tactics again? We'll have to wait and see, but given the history of woke, democrats, it is a very good bet that they will. Meanwhile, parents that speak at PTA meetings, Catholics, and MAGA supporters are all still terrorists (according to our government), and as a white male, I'm still a racist bigot. That is if you believe the Woke democrats.

As I pray for Israel each day, I also pray for our country. I pray we survive the biden crime family, and these woke democrats and their crooked election. I want to see America restored to greatness. Perhaps one day we can

127

hold the feet of dishonest democrats to the fire. If that can happen in a local election for mayor in Bridgeport, CT, it can happen elsewhere too!

William N. Bender

REFLECTION 23:

I Am Now Ashamed to be a Black, Trans, Female!

William N. Bender, Ph.D.

O K, OK! I know I've played with the humor of an old white guy like me "identifying" as a black trans female before. I covered that idea early in this Diary, and if I identify as a black trans female, I can get me some government benefits. Well, all kidding aside, I could use the money. Who couldn't?

Still, I don't want to be boring here, so I'll just say that this black, trans female thing is relevant again this week (November 8, 2023) for one reason. The Trans Manifesto was leaked! Finally! Now we get the news that we should have had nearly a year ago.

Now You might remember last March, when a white (not black) trans, biological female person decided to shoot up a Christian school, the Covenant School, that she, or he, or whatever had previously attended. It happened in Nashville, TN, and three children and three adults at the school were killed by this particular trans crazy person. Now I have a PH.D. in crazy, or at least, in a relevant field here, and I do know all about crazy. I know it when I see it.

Speaking of crazy, My OCD wife recently commented. "In every marriage there is someone who stacks the dishwasher perfectly like a

Scandinavian architect, and someone else who stacks it like a racoon on meth." What exactly, was she trying to say?

But back to the Nashville shooting. In the aftermath, everyone wanted to know her, his, or whatever's motives. Why would this tranny person believe it necessary to kill Christians? It was well documented at the time that the shooter had written a manifesto, and that his, or her, or whatever's reasons for the shooting were plainly stated. However, that manifesto was withheld from the public, for no reason whatsoever, or at least no reason that anyone could explain. Who ever thought that the reasons for a mass shooting need to be kept secret by our media? Well, anyone who thinks the media is basically biased. Anyone like me, for example.

However, truth eventually comes out. This past week several pages of that manifesto were leaked, and it proved that the motivations for the killing of several white children and adults were hatred of white "crackers" and "white privilege." This thing was as hateful as many of us suspected. In short, it showed all the hatred of most woke leftist democrats.

"Wanna kill all you little crackers!!! Bunch of little f***ers, w/ your white privileges."

"I hope I have a high death count."

These are the exact quotes according to a Fox news report, and the three leaked pages have been verified as authentic. Of course, many news agencies (CNN, ABC, NBC) didn't even report on this story at all, which one would expect from the dishonest mainstream media. I mean those sources will not report on anything that goes against the narrative of the victimhood of "poor, innocent trans people who are victims of society."

In the wake of this tragedy last March, the entire basis for stories about this in the mainstream media involved not violence by trans people against white Christians, but rather, gun control! Fox news also pointed out that, had the shooting been perpetrated by a "Republican, or a conservative leaning shooter," the shooter's motives would have been central to the story *from the first news reports. Mainstream news agencies love to report on white perpetrators of mass shootings, particularly when victims are black, or trans, or gay or whatever. However, in this Tennessee case, because the shooter was a female trans, the motives, while plainly stated by the shooter, had to be kept secret! Hard to imagine a supposed news agency, or for that matter, the policing agencies, choosing to keep secret the motives of a shooter, any shooter, that kills six people, but our mainstream media is so dishonest that such was the case. Given the political correctness demanded of our policing agencies in the nation today, the police also chose to keep this manifesto a secret.*

Tsumani --T is silent; Honest -- H is silent; Psychology -- P is silent; Knife --K is silent; Wife – Husband is silent. Any story where white Christians are the victims – Mainstream media is silent.

So it is now proven; this Tennessee shooting was very clearly a hate crime. It was a shooting by a white biological female, a trans person, who herself, himself, themselves, or whatever, had enjoyed the presumed white privilege. This hate crime was perpetrated against white adults and children simply because those victims were white Christians. Again, the dishonesty of the mainstream press is so apparent in this example, that one has to wonder how many of the things said about the political perspectives of the press are true? Will the mainstream press actually ignore important news, or aspects of news stories that don't fit their political perspectives? It did in this case.

Never, ever trust the mainstream press. Most of what they report is biased, slanted, propaganda, for woke democrats.

I generally choose to believe a news story, when I see it in multiple conservative news sources such as FreeSpoke, NewsMax, Fox News, etc., and those sources collaborate each other. Ultimately, I think things are actually proven only when hard evidence is presented and examined in a court of law.

I note that I haven't heard the words "hate crime" from any news source as yet, relative to this Nashville shooting. I guess things are only a hate crime, when they are done by white, conservatives. Who knew?

So what can I, and you, and other conservative Christians do about this? I should note that this exact question was asked in my Christian Tuesday Morning Coffee Group, just this week. Here's a Christian answer.

We can Pray. Pray that Jesus' love can be made real in our lives, even as we white Christian conservatives are victimized by hate from woke democrats. Others will see that love, if we can follow Jesus' teachings.

We should Pray that we can show that love, and the power of that love, rather that choose to be victims of this hatred.

Pray that each of us has the strength to do love, as Jesus did, in the face of evil.

Also, once the prayers are said, and our talk with God has been accomplished, we can write, and we can talk, we can support each other, and we can communicate our concerns to others. Moreso than ever, I invite all who may read this Diary to pray and then to communicate!

After your prayers for these victims, and this shooter, share your thoughts on this shooting and this dishonest press with me, with your local newspaper in a letter to the editor. Then send that letter to your Congressman. At some point, our nation has to become honest with itself in matters of this nature, and that is more likely when we communicate our concerns, as conservative Christians. At some point, Christians simply have to wake up.

Finally, do share this diary with others. I sincerely apologize for the self-serving nature of that request, but I still want each of you to send this Diary along to whomever you wish. When the question "what can I do" was asked just this past Tuesday morning, I didn't give that answer to my friends. I didn't say, write your Congressman, and pass this Diary along! But I should have.

So I am now, humbly asking; Please send this Diary—any part of it, or all of it, to any other Conservative Christians who may be interested. Get emails of other folks who might like to get these reflections and send them to me; I'll add them to the email list.

Of course, if this is too much to read, or for any other reason, I'll remove anyone from that email list at any time, upon their request. And if I get such a request, I will not be offended by that. I will respect the wishes of everyone in that regard.

Still, in an earlier Diary entry I pointed to the strength of communication—the power of the Committee's of Correspondence of the 1770s. Those groups helped organize the American public, helping prepare them for the American Revolution. In some states those early Committees helped form new state Congresses that governed our nation during the Revolution. I sincerely hope that there will be no need for another Revolution in our country—and yes, I've discussed that previously in this Diary as well.

Still, I truly believe that if Christians remain silent in the face of actual hate crimes against conservatives, Christians, Republicans, and all whites, etc., then we are not living up to our Christian duty.

I might also point out that while Jesus was accused of many things, he was never, ever, not once, accused of remaining silent in the face of evil that injured other people.

Let me use his strength, and his love, to speak loudly in the face of the evil of our ever woke government. I pray, and I believe, that my actions are consistent with his will.

William N. Bender, Ph.D.

REFLECTION 24:

Do Christians Really Hate People?

William N. Bender, Ph.D.

I must have missed the memo, here. I've always believed that when I felt hatred in my heart, for anyone, even my enemies, I was not living up to the example of Jesus. I missed the memo that said Christians should hate people. Still, that concept of Christian hatred is right there in the ever biased mainstream media, for all to see. This morning's headline from something called the Princess Free Zone is as follows:

"Right Wing Christians Really Hate Their Neighbors": US Supreme Court Ruling Threatens Mass Deportation of Immigrant 'Dreamer' Children.

Do Christians really hate? Is that the story our mainstream press pushes on the American people? The answer seems to be yes. Of course, I looked up the source of this headline, that somehow appeared in my news feed. It turns out that the Princess Free Zone is a blog written by Michele Yulo, to "offer an alternative to all things princess for little girls by addressing issues of gender and gender stereotyping." That should be enough to explain the overt dishonesty in proclaiming that Christians hate anyone. Other stories on the blog include: "My father's affair, and our other brother" and "Gender Stereotyping Begins in Infancy." So much for Ms. Yulo and her perspectives. While no-one is for harsh gender stereotyping, Christians do stand for *honesty, and this headline above was nothing more than dishonest clickbait. I don't wish to label Ms. Yulo as dumb, but clearly she is either very dumb or very dishonest. In other words, we have the ramblings of another woke, gender-infatuated leftist here, who is probably in a great deal of pain for one reason or another, and has an axe to grind (though, again, she might just be dumb as lumber!).*

At the post office today I saw a blond screaming into an envelope. I asked what she was doing and she said, "I'm sending a voice mail, DUH!"

Still, this issue of how mainstream media presents Christians is heady stuff for any conservative Christian. It seems that Christians are as hated by the mainstream press as white males, or conservatives, or Republicans, or Catholics! We see terms like, "Christian Nationalist" or "Christian Privilege" which as far as I can determine is an offshoot of the imaginary "White Privilege." As you may know I've deal with that imaginary concept before.

White Privilege = Success resulting from good parenting, education, and a strong work ethic.

Anyone who has those things, regardless of their skin color, will usually succeed in life, and anyone who doesn't will have less success. Here are a few folks who specifically benefited from this white privilege.

Colon Powel	*Senator Tim Scott*	*Dr. Thomas Sowell*
Condoleezza Rice	*Candace Owen*	*Dr. Martin Luther King*
Jessie Jackson	*Andrew Young*	

This list could go on, but you get the point; all these folks benefited greatly from white privilege, and all are Black. Skin color is irrelevant to white privilege—the very term doesn't make sense, if one is honest. Still, honesty, and integrity are not strong points for the woke left.

If you think some of my posts are ridiculous, you should see some of my life choices!

But what about Christian privilege? That's another term tossed about by the woke left democrats today, and it seems to aim directly at we Christian conservatives. Should we be worried about that? We'll let's remember the old adage:

*****Sticks and stones can break my bones, but words can absolutely destroy my life.*****

Sorry, I know that's not exactly the way that saying used to go, but in today's wired world, with the internet spreading so much info that simply isn't true, the statement above is much more accurate than the older saying.

When I looked the term "Christian Privilege" up, I was taken to de Tocqueville's writings from 1832. That French political scientist was studying the politics on the "new country" of America in the 1830s, and noted that while religion was separated from the state (i.e. no church was supported by state funds or taxes), it still held perhaps the greatest influence over the population. He considered religion the primary political institution in America because of the huge influence Christianity had culturally.

Fast forward to today, and this dominance of Christianity in our culture impacts everyone. Thus, in today's world, one is presumed to be advantaged socially and economically, if one is a Christian, in a county in which Christian thought dominates.

This, like many lies and half-truths, sounds reasonable, unless you honestly look at the issue. Again, honesty is not a characteristic of the woke left, but we'll make every effort to be honest here, so here's the reality. Christianity no longer dominates our culture. At least since the cultural revolution of the 1960s and 1970s, Christianity has played far less of a role in our society than it did for the first 200 years of American history.

In America today I know of no Christian that would argue that Christian thought or perspectives dominate political discourse; in fact, most

Christians would argue the exact opposite of that. Most Christians today feel that secular humanism, or political wokeness, or the hate-filled, anti-American rants of pink headed members of Antifa or BLM dominate culture today. Most conservative Christians view the democratic party as the vehicle of woke evils, if not the root of such evil. Democrats have become the force representing every special interest in the nation, from the trans movement and gender free bathrooms, to hate-filled anti-American protesters such as BLM or the Palestinians who just last week stormed Grand Central Station to presumably attack several police officers there. While Christian thought may have been dominant in 1832, to suggest it is a dominant political force today is foolish.

You can't control who walks into your life, but you can control which window you throw them out of!

And what about Christian Nationalism? What exactly is it? Is it the Christianity that fostered a republic that actually values the individual, even as Jesus valued every individual? Is Christian Nationalism the sense that our nation would be better off if, as Christians, we learned to value our adversaries in political debate, rather than vilifying them with names such as deplorable? We'll go to Wikipedia and take a look.

Christian Nationalism is defined as a type of religious nationalism that is affiliated with Christianity, in which the end goal is to achieve a Christian theocracy within a society.

On the face of it, this doesn't sound too bad, and I'd like to live in a country in which Christian love, tolerance, and valuing of every individual's opinion was the rule rather than the exception. However, history teaches us that Christian theocracies generally turn into very un-Christian tyranny. The old adage, "power corrupts, and absolute power corrupts absolutely" is accurate when Christianity overtly dominates government. The dominance of the Roman Catholic church for 1000 years, led to such a horrid corruption of Christianity that a complete Reformation was necessary, to get back to Jesus's teachings. Of course, later Protestant theocracies were likewise corrupted by *power crazed folk. John Calvin's Geneva under his reformed Christianity was turned into a horrid, hate-filled city. Under Calvin's reforms shows and entertainments were expressly forbidden by their religion, and for more than two hundred years there was not a single musical instrument allowed in the city of Geneva. Power corrupted absolutely in Geneva, and Calvin ended up burning his political opponents at the stake, literally. Just like today's woke leftists would like to burn we deplorables.*

As another example, when the Puritan movement, an offshoot of the Christian Reformation, hit North America, that religion dominated politics in Massachusetts. Their perceptions of God ruled the government for a while (1620 – 1700, or so), and it was horrible. Puritanism was particularly strong in Salem, where 19 "witches" were hanged by those Puritan theologians, and another was crushed to death. Everyone spent the year 1692 horrified, not leaving their homes, least they meet a witch, or worse yet, be accused themselves. In today's world, one can either choose to believe in witches riding sticks in the night, or rightly state that 20 innocent people were condemned by an overly religious government. In all over 200 citizens were accused and arrested for being witches, based on what was called "spectral" evidence which was essentially an accusation by a teenager. These young girls believed that only they could see a "specter" or ghost of a witch. Clearly, theocracies lead to tyranny, and I'm pretty sure I don't want to live in a Christian theocracy. So I guess by that aspect of the definition, I'm not a Christian Nationalist.

Still, if you read on in the Wiki about Christian Nationalism, you get to things like redefining the USA as exclusively a Christian nation, and comparisons with hard right politics. Some even argued that the January 6 riot at the Capital was a "Christian Nationalist" movement—though actual interviews with participants suggest they were motivated by the belief that a Presidential election was "stolen" and that Trump was rightfully, our President.

Personally, I do recognize the fact that our nation was founded by Christians, as did de Tocqueville, way back in the 1830s. Virtually all of our founding fathers attended one Christian church or another on a regular basis. However, given that our founding fathers were also educated in the "Age of Reason" they did not write religious requirements into our founding documents. They were not about to create a Christian theocracy. Rather, their goal in those documents was to maximize the value of, and the potential of, the individual citizen; to maximize freedom within the law, and to limit the power of the federal government. That too, apparently, is Christian Nationalism, according to some.

In short, once you look at the definition of Christian Nationalism, you find out that the definition is so inclusive of all right leaning perspectives that it is virtually meaningless. Of course, to the woke left, this very vagueness allows the use of this term when they wish to demonize someone of a different political belief. Using imprecise language when demonizing one's political opponents is par for the course by woke leftists today, so we'll just let our comment on this misleading, ill-defined term speak for itself. As to the name calling of the woke left, at least we Christian deplorables are in good company.

Jesus, in his day, was called a drunkard, a sinner, demon-possessed, and (horror of horrors) even a Samarian! He never bothered to refute any of these terms with his critics.

We shouldn't either. I will respond to bad, dishonest arguments, because not responding in the face of evil, allows evil to triumph. Still, I won't waste time trying to convince woke leftists of their many errors in judgement. I'll merely write my beliefs about those terms and political ideas, and laugh a bit at the violent extreme hatred of the left.

Those poor woke leftists are going to give themselves a coronary, if they don't lighten up a bit.

If I got a dollar for every time I thought about you, I'd start thinking about you.

Further, I'd suggest that all conservatives just be good Jesus followers. Let's speak up in the face of evil, and then let's pray for our country, our enemies, and for Israel, even while we note that those with weak political beliefs tend to call their opponents nasty names. For now, we'll just leave it at that.

William N. Bender, Ph.D.

REFLECTION 25:

Salem Witch Trials, and Witch Hunts Today

William N. Bender, Ph.D.

I just finished reading a book by Bill O'Reilly and Matin Dugard, called Killing the Witches. I love the books that these two authors write together—it's called the "Killing Series." Various titles include "Killing Lincoln" "Killing Kennedy" "Killing Patton" "Killing the Mob," and I think my favorite is "Killing Jesus." These books are well researched history and present highly accurate stories on these and many other topics.

I found "Killing Jesus," and the others to be highly interesting. I'd recommend all of these books to history buffs, and in particular, every Christian should read, "Killing Jesus."

Still this is more than a book recommendation. I bring this book, "Killing the Witches" up for a reason in the context of this Diary of a Deplorable. If you've read some or most of my first 24 Reflections from the Diary, you know that I am very concerned with our current woke culture, the dishonesties involved with "cancelling" someone and how our mainstream press as well as our nation's corporate giants foster these highly negative realities. Imagine my surprise when I found that these two authors share my beliefs, and my disrespect for the woke, cancel culture. Here's a direct quote from that book.

"Today, there is a new kind of witch hunt. Accusations mean guilt. The press drives that every day. No one is executed, but lives are ruined in terrible ways."

O'Reilly and Dugard begin with the Salem witch trials of 1692, along with other witch trials from 1650 onward. They then move into discussions of our Founding Fathers, and the struggle to free our nation from Great Britian. They make the historic case, accurately I might add, that much of the struggle that led to the American Revolution involved freedom from state sponsored religion—specifically the "paying of taxes" to the Church of England—called the Anglican Church here in the colonies in the 1700s. They point to the relationship between Ben Franklin—a man whom I greatly admire—and Cotton Mather—a man I do not admire. Mather was an Anglican preacher who was instrumental in the Salem witch trials. They then discuss modern demonic possession, with a historic description of the events that were the basis for the book and movie, The Exorcist in the 1970s. Even today, many Christians believe demonic possession is real, a belief shared by Islam, many African religions and Voodoo Priests throughout the Caribbean.

During those famous witch trials near Boston in 1692, if a teenaged girl shouted that she saw you, me, or anyone else in "spectral" form (i.e. a ghostly projection of someone), then that person could be considered a witch. If the "specter" harmed the girl herself or someone else, such "spectral evidence" was considered enough to "prove" someone was a witch. On such evidence, 19 persons were hung—mostly women, and one man was crushed to death. Over 200 persons were accused of being witches based on "spectral evidence" that nobody else could see!

It clearly wasn't the best choice to live in Salem, MA in 1692. These folks simply lived in the wrong place—a place dominated by well meaning Christians, who held absolute power. I believe in Jesus, and want Christians to be a serious influence in society—the salt of the Earth. But, like the founding fathers of America, I do not want any religious belief to exclusively hold political power—again, absolute power corrupts absolutely.

Stop complaining about your life! There are literally people living today in California!

The Reverend Cotton Mather argued for the use of such "spectral evidence"—I'd call it "imaginary evidence" in his efforts to "get the Devil out of Salem", and again, he and the Puritans held absolute power in Salem and much of Boston, only 25 miles away. In many ways, Cotton Mather was directly responsible for those 20 deaths, and the 200 lives, many of which were destroyed, based on imaginary evidence, and an accusation of girls, some of whom were as young as 11. His grave is in Copp's Hill Burying Ground in Boston. I'd like to visit that historic grave someday, even knowing that Mather led one of the blackest periods in colonial American history.

The best epitaph I've ever seen on a gravestone: " I wouldn't be where I am today without my wife!"

Now, I'm completely against holding historical figures responsible for our moral values today. That is why I think our nation is stupid to rename military bases just because the namesake of those facilities owned slaves. I don't think it fair to judge historic figures by our standards today. History records that Mather really believed he was doing the work of Jesus, when he argued for use of spectral evidence. I mentioned Salem, MA in my last reflection as an example of a Christian theocracy. When Christians (or any other humans) hold absolute power, that power will usually corrupt absolutely. It did when well-meaning Puritans ruled in Salem, MA in 1692, and many innocent people were wrongfully put to death or imprisoned for being witches. This is one of the best reasons for the separation of church and state.

But does this give us an example of how to combat the witch hunts of today? The book presents several examples of media figures wrongfully accused of being racists, and having their lives destroyed. This is the woke culture of the left at its finest; its most dishonest. Attempting to silence reasonable discussion simply because it presents conservative views, as woke liberal democrats are doing today, is simply wrong, and attempts to then discredit *or cancel the conservative speaker, many times the Christian conservative speaker, are simply evil. It most often involves unproven allegations or accusations—just like the spectral evidence in the Salem witch trials—and the effect is the same. Innocent people have their lives destroyed by falsehoods.*

I truly believe that, as American Christian conservatives wake up, the woke leftist, and their lap dog—the mainstream media—will be completely embarrassed by what they allowed themselves to become. We now know of multiple instances in which our government colluded with our nation's press and big tech companies to disallow honest (many times totally accurate) perspectives from the conservative right—the hunter biden laptop story, the Russian collusion with Trump story, the lab leak theory for the origins of Covid. All of these stories were dismissed by our woke press—all were, in fact true. At some point even those folks who voted for biden in 2020 will have to admit that our world is much less safe and stable than it was under a much stronger president, President Trump. One of these days, even the woke leftists will realize the abject failure of liberal policies concerning the open southern border, or the failure of wind energy, or the myth that electric vehicles will replace gas cars within our lifetime. Indeed, one of these days….

It's been "one of those days," for the last 3 years or so. Just about the same time that slow joe has been in office!

Well, here we are. The biden crime family is still in power, though Republican Congressmen believe an impeachment trial of slow joe may begin as soon as the Spring of 2024. How long must honest conservatives endure under these woke leftists, these dishonest, repugnant witch hunters, who are ever ready to destroy lives, simply because someone disagrees with their political perspective? I long for a day, when the Christian Right will rise up, and perhaps that time is near. Tucker Carlson often says that many of these issues will explode with the coming 2024 election, and as of today, Trump is leading sloe joe in the polls by one to five percentage points. We'll see.

I hope to see Trump, or someone with his strength elected the next time around. I hope to see names of military bases revert back to historic names, and I hope to see justice done to all those dishonest leftists democrats who lied outright to the American people—Shift, Crooked Hillary, Comey, slow joe, and his whole crime family, obummer, and other leftists liars who perpetuate the witch hunts of today. These people should be behind bars, and I want to see justice done. I'm reminded here of a quote from Dr. Martin Luther King, made famous when he was in jail.

Justice delayed is justice denied. *(Dr. Martin Luther King: Letter from a Brimingham Jail).*

As Christian conservatives, we can not let the witch hunters of today in either the government or the mainstream media practice their axiom of "guilty until proven innocent." As Americans who love this country, we cannot let that woke leftist's view win.

William N. Bender

PS   Again, all Christians should read "Killing Jesus," and "Killing the Witches," by the authors above. These are great books and I promise you will learn a lot.

PSS   As always, pray for our country. Pray for the love of Jesus to spread out over this land, and all around our world, and always, always, pray for Israel.

REFLECTION 26:

A Thanksgiving Prayer

William N. Bender, Ph.D.

So Thanksgiving rolled around again, and I have chosen to become younger with each succeeding year (and I wish myself good luck with that one!). Still, mine was a blessed Thanksgiving, as I hope yours was. I got to see my wonderful granddaughters, when my son and his lovely wife visited, and on the Friday after Thanksgiving, I held another Thanksgiving!

I have a group of friends that my wife and I have assisted a bit (and a number of you guys who read this Diary have helped them too!). Some of those guys had horrid childhoods, and have virtually no family, and thus no Thanksgiving tradition at all. Several of those folks have had horrid challenges in their childhood, but this group is now succeeding in their lives. It is a blessing to me and my wife to help them rebuild their lives, using funds from The John Bender Foundation (which many of you contribute too—and thank you for that).

Thanksgiving—a day to gather your dysfunctional family for a meal, and hope the cops don't get called!

For some in this group, that sentiment was all too accurate! Still, we got together that Friday and held another Thanksgiving! It was a blessed day, for a variety of reasons. Of course, the food was copious, and delicious, and like many Americans, I disrespected my own body, and ate way too much!

146

My body should be a temple, but it's really more like a bar and grill!

Anyway, we had people over for our One-Day-Late Thanksgiving. As I've often said, this group blesses Wify and I at least as much as we bless them. Thus, I was more than happy to write a Thanksgiving Prayer for that meal. It was read that day, by one of my "borrowed Kids" Ben, a sixth grade friend. He practiced it several times and did a great job on the Prayer.

Because it is often wise to step away from politics on holidays, I now present this prayer for you. Wishing you the best Thanksgiving, and a wonderful, soon to come Christmas Season.

A Thanksgiving Prayer

God, today we come together as friends and family, around this table, to give thanks.

You created billions of stars, and millions upon millions of galaxies that we see each night, and you placed them all in the heavens, and yet you know me and everyone at this table by name. For this, we give thanks.

Everyone at this table is succeeding in life today in some way, and for this we give thanks.

Each of us will face challenges in our life, and we understand that these will make us stronger, if we bring our concerns to you, and for this we give thanks.

Now as we move into the holy season of Christmas, we understand that the manger led directly to the cross, and that on that cross, your son died for our sins. And for that, the greatest gift of all, we give thanks.

Let us be mindful of that great gift throughout this holy season, and as we eat this food, and enjoy the friendship, laughter, and love around this table, let us give thanks.

Let us understand in a new and profound way, that all good things come from you.

And on this Thanksgiving Day, let us be ever thankful for all of these blessings, the food on this table, and all the friends around it.

Amen

REFLECTION 27:

Biden Presidency is a "Dumpster fire".

William N. Bender, Ph.D.

A fter I completed my Sunday School lesson this fine Sunday morning I was greeted with the following headline.

Earth to Democrats: Biden Presidency is a Dumpster Fire. How many warnings do you need?

Imagine my surprise! This was actually in the mainstream media! While I agree completely with this, I was still surprised to see this headline from the mainstream media, since they have, as a group, been all in with slow joe and the entire biden crime family for many years now. This story was, of course, an opinion piece published in USA Today. Still, it is the mainstream media finally acknowledging that this is a failed presidency, and said presidency is quickly leading to a failed country. You may have noticed, I share that opinion, as evidenced in this Diary.

Now, as Tucker Carlson recently stated, it is difficult to admit our President is demented. Like Carlson, I often use that term for slow joe, but I do not take pleasure in it. Still, he is both demented, and a criminal. These are facts, but each time I write those out it hurts me a bit to have to admit that our country has come to this—that so many woke liberals are so very dishonest, so as to vote for this man. In fact, according to the national polls, a not-insignificant minority of Americans are intending to vote for him *again. I do not understand this, but it really gives me no pleasure to point to his incapacity to do the job of national and world leader. We have two wars, economic hardships, and failed leadership with our ongoing problems in this nation, largely because of joe biden and his cronies. We simply have to do better.*

Still, the headline above, and the fact that this reality of biden's failed presidency was finally acknowledged in the mainstream press, do give me hope. Further, I take much hope from the polls that, almost universally suggest that President Trump will, once again, be in the White House— that is of course, unless the woke liberal democrats manage to steal another election.

While completing a Bible study recently, I found a verse that, I believe completely describes woke liberal democrats. Now many of us believe that the Bible really does answer most questions, and as I wonder how anyone could still believe in the biden Presidency, this verse from second Thessalonians helped me understand a bit.

They did not receive the love of truth, that they might be saved. And for this reason God will send them strong delusion, that they should believe the lie, that they all might be condemned who did not believe the truth. *II Thessalonians 2 10-12.*

In the modern (read woke liberal) frame of perception, truth is relative (I'm reminded here of the famed quote from Pontius Pilate: "What is truth?"). And when truth is relative, then one's reality simply becomes anything one wishes to perceive. From that frame of reference, one can believe the lies from the White House: that "Bidenomics really is working, to make our economic lives easier for all Americans," and another myth, "The southern border is secure!" and another; "biden won the election in 2020."

Each time a woke democrat is found guilty of stuffing ballot boxes, or the result of a local election that resulted in a democratic victory is overturned by the courts, the case that Trump won the 2020 election becomes somewhat stronger. Moreover, it is clear that biden supporters do not love truth, so they will choose to believe strong delusions—the lie—and will be condemned because they did not follow the truth. I wrote on this earlier in the Diary—those woke liberal democrats—drank the Kool-aide!

Jan 6 will go down in history as the day the federal government staged a riot, to cover up the fact that the left stole an election.

I can't wait to see if opinion pieces such as the article mentioned above become more common as the 2024 election approaches. In fact, I can't imagine a weaker presidential candidate for President Trump to face in 2024 than slow joe. It is even possible to believe that biden may be impeached in early 2024. Of course, I must remind myself and all of us, that the term "impeachment" means to "stand trial for office," it does not mean to be "removed from office." I think it likely that slow joe will be impeached in early 2024—as many Republican investigators have stated. I do not think he will be removed from office, as there are simply too many dishonest democrats in the Senate, including, unfortunately, two from my home state of Georgia. Still, when one's political enemies are heading off a cliff (by selecting slow joe as the democratic candidate for 2024) perhaps we Conservative Christians should let them keep running for the cliff! I'm reminded of a saying attributed to Napoleon Bonaparte.

"Never interrupt your enemy when they are making a mistake."
Napoleon Bonaparte

What we can say for sure is that something, some history changing event, is sure to happen in the coming election. We have two of the oldest men ever likely to win nomination. What happens if either dies while running? What happens if half of the country chooses to believe that the election is stolen again? This promises to be interesting, so I'll continue looking to see if the democrats are really waking up to the dumpster fire of the slow joe, demented, presidency. May God save us all, from this horridly bad leadership.

Dr. William N. Bender

REFLECTION 28:

Paying for Appeasement: Obummer's Guilt

William N. Bender, Ph.D.

On November 7, Senator Tom Cotton spoke in the senate of the guilt of our former democratic president bareck obummer (yes, that's intentional disrespect; Think I'll just use his original name Barry, from now on), for empowering Iran, during his recent presidential administration. Barry was the one who essentially gave Iran nuclear capability, and while Trump in his White House stay had enforced economic sanctions against Iran, slow joe has reversed that policy. While sanctions are still in place, they are not enforced, as reported by many media outlets.

So under Trump, Iran had essentially no money. Now under slow joe it does.Remember that slow joe released funds for Iran, and some of those went to Hamas. Recall also, that our "humanitarian aid" going into Gaza now, is largely controlled by Hamas, since they are the only real power in the Gaza Strip. Thus, Iran is funding Hamas terror, and according to Senator Cotton, Barry is directly responsible for the Hamas attacks that led to the current war.

Just as a reminder, 30 Americans lost their lives on Oct. 7, 2023, when Hamas killed some 1200 persons in the original attack. Many Americans are still hostages of Hamas, if they are still alive at all, and we have both Barry and slow joe to thank for this. This is what appeasement looks like.

As a historian, I can't help but note that this is history repeating itself. In 1938, England, then a world power, appeased Hitler's Germany, by giving large chunks of Europe to Germany, simply because Hitler made up some excuse to "take" parts of Austria and most of Czechoslovakia. Thus, England essentially "gave" Hitler what that idiot dictator wanted, to achieve "Peace in our time!" As a result, Hitler knew he was dealing with cowardly idiots, and kept on taking land in Europe. As a result of England's appeasement of Hitler, we had WW II, and over 40 million deaths. We should have learned then that appeasement doesn't work. In that war, Hitler conquered most of Europe, including France, much of Poland, and the Balkin States. America had to step in and save England, France, most of Europe, and the rest of the world. Simple rule from history: appeasement leads to war.

Had a friend in France block me. We were discussing French culture and history, when he challenged me and asked, "Who won the first tour de France?" Apparently, Germany's 5th Panzer Division was not the answer he was looking for.

I'll also note, and I have previously in this diary, that most democrats seem to believe in appeasement as a viable political strategy. Both Barry and slow joe simply ignored it when Putin, the current dictator in Russia took Chechnya, so now, Putin is trying to take more land in the Ukraine. This is appeasement—giving land to a petty, power-hungry dictator, and expecting one such "gift" of land to stop the dictator's aggression. I'm sure that when Barry gave a nuclear deal to Iran, he actually believed that appeasement would stop Iran's bad actions. Again, the lesson from history: Appeasement leads to war.

According to Senator Cotton, Barry cut a deal to empower Iran, ran from Iraq, allowed Syria to disintegrate into chaos, and all of these factors empowered Iran, and caused the current war. Because I love history, I tend to have a long memory. I remember when Barry was first elected to the White House, and he made his "Muslim Tour." During that series of visits to Muslim dictatorships or Kingdoms, he bowed to various other Kings, and consistently apologized for America. It pissed me off then, and it still pisses me off. Still, those apologies didn't seem to make muslims love us any more. So sorry, barry, but your leadership was almost as much of a disaster as the current administration.

As earlier sections of this Diary show, I've been worried that America will be drawn into this war—a fact that has now been realized. American bases throughout the region are routinely attacked by missiles from Iran, and America is acting only defensively, in shooting them down. American naval power is also shooting down weapons heading to Israel, so we are already in this war. How long will it be before and American warship is hit and Americans die?

Oh, sorry. Thirty Americans have already died, but slow joe really doesn't seem to mind too much. Is he taking sedatives or simply wholly unaware? One has to wonder.

When I see a happy housewife on TV, joyfully using one cleaning product or another, I think about my wife, and the I want to buy the medications those TV wives use.

Well, some might say, let's wait and see where our current leadership, and the current policies of appeasement lead us. For those who know history, there is no need to wait. America needs a strong President, and our only real hope is that we get one in 2024.

Simple lesson here: Appeasement doesn't work; Barry and slow joe tried it, and their actions gave our enemies the power to begin a war in Israel—that is the message from Senator Cotton, and he is right on the money. As usual here, when we find something horrible in the world, we can usually thank a democrat!

As always, pray for America and Israel. On these two democracies, the future of mankind may rest. Pray for a new awareness of American Exceptionalism, and pray that woke democratic liberals finally see the errors that liberal policies like appeasement create. As we move into the most holy season of all, pray for peace.

While Prayer is the first, main answer, I also invite all to help circulate these Diary entries. With a growing, Conservative Christian voice, and with God's help, perhaps we can make a positive difference.

Dr. William N. Bender

PS: News just crossed my X account that a new independent audit of election results showed that many Republican ballots in Arizona were left uncounted. With each of these verified reports, it seems somewhat more likely that a Trump victory in 2020 may have been overturned by election fraud.

PSS: I'm seeing increasing numbers of stories about muslims throughout the middle east converting to Christianity. I've also read about "appearances" of Jesus in various muslim gatherings. I pray that this is so. Only the love that Jesus taught us will get the world out of this mess, but that fact does not relieve Christians of responsibility. We must show that his love is simply a better way to live. I'm sure this Diary will include some thoughts on these appearances of Jesus soon.

REFLECTION 29:

A Horrid War in Israel

Dr. William N. Bender

Note: *This Diary of a Deplorable is now shared rather widely in six states. Please continue to share these reflections with your friends and invite them to join the email list by sending me a request at **benderbilly53@gmail.com**. Maybe we conservative Christians can make a difference.*

As I write this Diary of a Deplorable reflection on December 4, 2023, Hamas has released 110 hostages, and still holds 137. To make that release of hostages happen, Israel suspended the war through a cease fire, which Hamas broke, as one might expect of those hate filled people. During the ceasefire, Hamas shipped in many more weapons, and used the time to rebuild their military force, so today, Israel has a much tougher job than previously.

Personally, I do not think it right to compliment Hamas on release of hostages, as some have done. I think they are animals for taking hostages to begin with, and for still holding 137 hostages captive. The world has now seen how Hamas raped, terrorized, and murdered some defenseless hostages, and while some say this is simply an act of war, that is not true. Even when Japan used suicide planes to kill American Navy personnel in WW II, and while Japan tortured and starved American prisoners of war, our nation never once took hostages during that conflict. Germany gassed six million Jews, Homosexuals, Gypsies, and others, and America did not take hostages or retaliate in any similar fashion. As this proves, there really are rules even in warfare that honorable nations follow, and Hamas fighters are, in my opinion cowardly animals for taking hostages, raping females, beheading, and terrorizing innocents, including many children as young as 9 months old. Hamas literally burned children alive. Those fighters are pure evil.

As you can see, I'm pretty mad about this, and I think every Christian should be; every human being on the planet should be mad about this! Reading the news becomes more dangerous every day. I could easily give myself heart problems by being so mad, and so I have to use a bit of humor.

Best add ever on a flower shop window: "So how mad is your wife? Really?"

Again, some say Hamas is fighting a mighty military power in the only way possible, but once again, history proves that to be a lie. When Washington's army was reduced to some 5,000 soldiers during the early years of the American Revolution, that army faced down a powerful, 30,000 man force of British soldiers, all of whom were much better trained and much better equipped than the American force. America also had to contend with the British Navy, the most powerful military force in the world at that point. Still, Washington and his army fought honorably throughout that war. Unlike Hamas, they did not take hostages, and rape them, or burn them alive. In short, during every war in history, Americans have fought honorably, unlike the animals of Hamas and Hezbollah today.

I am glad to hear the news that Israel is using robots in the Hamas tunnels and essentially burying Hamas fighters alive—they deserve nothing less. I'm trying to "love my enemies" but some enemies make that harder than others.

My wife's gardening tip. When you bury your husband's body, make sure to cover it with endangered plant species. That way, it is illegal to dig up!

As I expected, America is taking a larger role in this war. American warplanes routinely bomb targets throughout the middle east, to protect American bases and ships that have come under attack. Just this morning the news presented the movement of American Marines into Syria from other bases in the region, in order to better protect Israel and American troops in that area. Iran has issued "warnings" to America, even while they continue to fund Hezbollah and Hamas, with American dollars given to them by slow joe biden and obummer in recent years.

Once again, Thank you Mr biden! You did that!

I continue to pray for Israel and America in this conflict. Ultimately, I pray for peace after the evils have been destroyed. I pray for better government in America, that we may, once again be a great nation, and not a cowardly banker for Iran, Hamas, and other evils of the world. Perhaps one day, we can, once again see America as a shinning light upon a hill.

One final prayer. As we move into the holy season of Christmas, I pray for myself, that I become stronger, in practicing the love of Jesus, and not the hatred I feel when I consider Hamas, slow joe, and other worldwide evils. It is my job, as Jesus taught, to become a better man through learning to love even my enemies. I need help there: I need prayers for that. So…

Season's Greetings! Here's wishing you a very happy, whatever doesn't offend you.

Just kidding; Christians say Merry Christmas! May this Christmas, more than any in recent history, be a time when love and peace take over the whole world. Jesus' love can make that happen, and I pray that I can help. Merry Christmas, everyone!

Dr. William N. Bender

REFLECTION 30:

A Beginning and An End

Dr. William N. Bender

Today is January 1, 2024! Happy New Year everyone. I haven't been writing much in the Diary in December, with holiday travel, etc. but I do hope everyone had a wonderful Christmas! As Christians we know that Jesus is born, and that brings hope into a bleak world. Also, I'm wishing everyone a happy new year. I'll have to begin this year with humor!

Santa hired a DEI consultant, and things began to happen! A "White Christmas" shall be called a "frozen rain, mid-winter celebration of indeterminate coloration," all snowmen will now be referred to as "snowpersons," all reindeer as "air freight specialists" and all elves as "Santa's size challenged assistants!"

Here's some news. This Diary entry—Reflection 30—will officially end this Diary. I've decided that I will look into getting this thing actually published, though it will probably be with a "vanity" press. Still, the messages herein are timely—and their shelf-life is limited. The Revolution which I believe is coming will take place within the next 12 months, as we come to a historic Presidential Election. Tucker Carlson is in agreement—as he often reflects on the topics I've discussed herein, he says he doesn't know what is going to happen, but he knows something huge is! I have to agree, and if this

Diary is to have an impact, I'll need to get it published right away. I know this thing is circulated fairly broadly now, but these messages need to be heard. I will continue to write these reflections and will continue to send them to each of you, but the first set of 30 Reflections—these 30 Reflections—should be available in book form, so I'll be looking into options. Please continue to circulate this as much as you can.

Of course those who know me know that I will rarely be quite (my wife, as it happens, has the same disability), so of course I'll keep writing this Diary and sending new Reflections out.

Wife said, "Women are better at multitasking than men!" So I tested that proposition. I replied. "OK. Sit down and shut up!" She couldn't do either one!

With that said, here's a wrap-up, of many of the things we have discussed.

On Reparations: *Idiots still continue to call for reparations. The Chicago Mayor—a leftist, Black democrat—called for "reparations" last week and argued that it would fight crime! That's something of a new argument, and will work to fight crime in Chicago every bit as much as gun control laws in places like LA, in California and Chicago, Washington, DC, and Detroit help reduce crime. These harsh gun control laws in those towns have certainly made them safe, right? Hopefully reparations will work every bit as well! (Are you trying not to laugh yet?).*

Just kidding—those cities with the harshest gun control laws in the nation, are also among the highest crime areas in the nation. Gun control does not decrease crime, and reparations will not work to reduce crime either. As Dr. Larry Elder said, reducing fatherlessness in the Black community, and effective policing will reduce crime—virtually nothing else will.

But my ancestor really was an indentured servant. I want my money too!

I Still Waiting: Where's My Money!

On LGBTQ+ + +: *proponents of LGBTQ still haven't found another sex choice when they undergo sex reassignment surgery, other than male and female. Facts are facts people, no matter how much you shout against them or ignore them. There is still only 2 sexes; Word!*

I'm very worried. In recent years, testicular injuries in women's sports have skyrocketed!

On Trump: *The more the left demonizes this guy the stronger he gets. Even the woke-left media is realizing this at this point. According to my Twitter news feed (Now X), half of Hollywood plans to leave the USA when Trump is reelected. It may hurt there delicate feelings when they discover, nobody cares if they leave! Just in the last couple weeks, Colorado has decided to remove Trump's name from the presidential ballot. As I said in a previous reflection—that's when the revolution begins. My brother, Jack, does not believe that a revolution is coming, and I hope he's right. He cites Biblical passages indicating God will handle this madness, as he often has in the past. Again, I believe he is right. I'll be praying that my actions—that this Diary among others, are consistent with God's will. Still, and as a Trans, Black, female, I'll be wearing that Trump Mugshot T Shirt, and fighting for Trump!*

Finally got what TRUMP stands for: Truth Really Upsets Most People!

On War in Israel: *The War continues to progress, with Israel beating back Hamas in the Gaza Strip, and America is still, on occasion, fighting to defend bases in Iran, and to knock missiles out of the air that are heading toward ships in that area. America hasn't yet been sucked into a wider war, but that possibility is still open. The good news is that Israel is winning on all fronts. May God bless Israel, and help them to victory.*

On The Hostages: *Hamas, those dear sweet people, have been so kind as to release a number of hostages. Of course, they still hold many, merely proving their barbarism, and they broke the long awaited cease-fire. The stories of how they treated hostages is, well, what would we expect from a* bunch of devout muslims! They raped, they tortured, they killed (did these caring, devote muslims all of a sudden run out of goats or something?). The world seems to have noticed the crimes against female hostages, and evidence of sexual horrors committed by Hamas emerges daily, but I'm more concerned with the overt hatred against all jews. Islam in this entire region is based on generational hatred—that is what is taught to children. Such hatred is not what Jesus stands for, and teaching such hatred to children is the biggest crime of islam. In such a society, one must expect what we have seen from Hamas, and the only correct response to a coiled rattlesnake like Hamas is to kill it, as Israel is now doing.

Missing someone is a terrible thing. Ask any sniper.

Recently, one released hostage female reported that it is a myth that "the Palestinian people do not support Hamas." She was personally imprisoned and terrorized, not by Hamas fighters, but by a family of Palestinians, prior to being released. She has now stated that the family believed in what Hamas had done, making them culpable if not as bad as Hamas. That bondage she endured was terrifying, but it was also probably the only reason she was not raped. Again, goats seem to be scarce in Gaza. I pray Israel cleans these vermin out; the world will be a better place without them. I also pray that one day, peace and the love of Jesus will reign in that land. Today it does not: islam does, and that is an ugly, hate filled religion. I've read the verses in the unholy karan that are simply filled with hatred. You should too. Do not believe that this is a religion of peace, as is sometimes claimed.

On the biden crime family: The US House of Representatives has uncovered solid evidence of biden's crimes over the decades, and is moving toward impeachment this Spring. As I've said before, the Republicans in that chamber are doing their job, and I commend them. Of course, the department of Injustice announced new indictments against dear old hunter, and of course, that effectively "Protects" him from further investigation by the committees in the House of Representatives. This is dishonest government at its worst.

God, Grant me the serenity to accept the people I cannot change, the courage to change direction when I see them coming, and the wisdom to not smack some sense into them when I cannot avoid them. Amen

On the Economy: *Slow joe and his lying cronies continue to tell us all that the American economy is doing great, while he continues to fight against using our natural resources such as abundant coal and oil and natural gas. Everyone realizes that wind power is a joke and there is not enough electricity to power the EVs that slow joe wants us to drive. I really think this demented president believes his own lies; I don't know about the rest of the damocrats. Still, like most Americans....*

I am in an abusive relationship with the cost of living.

Democrats are so kind! They will give you the shirt off my back.

On the World Stage: *The world still laughs at America, and should slow joe be impeached and removed from office, we'll have kamilla! What a joy that will be. No real improvement at all. This really is the first time in history when both a president and a vice president were completely incoherent most of the time. China is gearing up for war, according to many sources in the Pentagon and Intelligence community, and will probably start by taking Tiawan back. After all, Putin has grabbed land, why shouldn't China? No one really thinks that with America's current, incredibly weak leadership, we would do anything about it, do they? Still, there may be a war with China, or Iran, or North Korea in our future, so for Americans, let's just keep voting for, these demented, language-challenged presidents!*

So what is one to do? I'll do what I know works. I'll pray, I'll write, I'll read and reflect, and when I can, I'll speak on these topics. I'll do it all with love (as best I can) and with humor. Convincing stupid people they are stupid is rarely a win-win proposition, but maybe a few Reflections can motivate a few like minded people to begin to take some action. If you are reading this, please share it with a conservative Christian friend. I'd urge you all to take whatever other actions you can, too. As Edmund Burke once said,

Evil wins when good people stay silent.

As I said on July 4, 2023, I will remain silent no more. I'll write, and laugh, and when the time comes join the fight. I'll try to live this coming year, this challenging year, this year of great danger, as Jesus would live. I'll try to love my enemies—I'm not good at that, but I'll try.

As for Me and My House: We Shall Serve the Lord.

I'll pray, write and think—I am good at that—and when possible I'll speak on these matters. Today, we begin 2024. Let the Games begin!

Godspeed, and may God Bless you during this coming, and very troubling year.

Dr. William Bender

Benderbilly53@gmail.com

REFLECTION 31:

I Damn Near Died

William N. Bender, Ph.D.

Note: *This is non- political reflection but this experience changed my life. I understand more about Jesus, now, so I thought it right to include this. I hope this is a blessing to you.*

It's Sunday night now (1/21/24) and I'm a bit bored. I'm also a writer, so I write. It's what I do. I've done 51 books (that I'm way too proud of) and 60 plus research articles that were published over the years. Still, I think that this might be the most important thing I've ever written. How's that for a build up? Anyway, this was how I spent my last nine days or so.

The PAIN came Friday, over a week ago (1/12/24), about 4:40 PM, as Wify and I were eating an early supper. Lower gut, left side; Google told me that was the wrong side for an appendix problem, so it had to be gas, right? So I just walked around the house a bit, and bent over holding my stomach when it seized me. PAIN clearly wanted my attention, and I wasn't going to give it the satisfaction. I was just waiting for the blinding FART that usually ended such gas pain. I would just walk and wait it out; I'm a big boy and I can do this. But then, PAIN got really, really pissed, and said to no one in particular, "Hold my beer."

My gut tightened; loosened; grabbed me, and bent me over. Me and PAIN were then into a test of wills! In 30 minutes or so Wify gave me 600 MG Ibuprophine. Only helped a bit. By then I was doubled over, bending with every step; walking around the house, and pushing on furniture to tighten and loosen shoulders and stomach muscles- we'll call that the idiot's PAIN relief strategy; doesn't work a bit, so please don't remember it, but that was my only choice—along with increasing PAIN. I'd been shooting prayers to my CREATOR off and on for an hour—these were not beautiful, lyrical well structured prayers—just a heart felt, "God help me get through this pain." I was pestering God to death, but, well, there it is.

But then I got really stupid, and took an Oxy (yes, my Dr. later chastised me about being dumb enough to take my wife's prescription PAIN meds). That didn't touch PAIN at all. So I walked in circles and shoved on some more furniture. Wify said how about going to the ER? Oh Hell no! I was still waiting for the FART to end all FARTS! The anticipated pressure wave would surely blow out windows! Should I be concerned with my neighbor's house across the street? You guys better be laughing by now, because this stuff is really, really embarrassing.

I remember in one silent "thought prayer," I actually prayed God would let me fart. I'd never done that before. I wanted a FART that would take the pain away. Still, after three hours and a few heavy drugs, it was decision time and yes, Wify had said that we should head for the hospital only 60 minutes into the ordeal, because she has a brain and was using it. By that point I wasn't. Big, strong, me! Apparently, I needed 2 more hours of the worst PAIN I've ever felt in my life! Of course, by then it wasn't my decision. I knew my battle with PAIN was no longer under my control, and I knew PAIN was winning. PAIN was on the ten yard line and charging to the endzone. So another uninspired prayer; "God please help me. I can't do this much longer." Then I doubled up again and PAIN charged forward some more, but God stepped in right about then. And It was Wify! God Bless her wonderfully twisted, determined, math-brained soul!

Hallelujah, Hallelujah! ***The brassiere came out of the drawer!***

Now, I should explain that things are getting serious in the Bender household when the brassiere comes out of the drawer! In my circle walking I could see Wify putting on the very thing she detested most, and it is very serious business when she puts on that bra. She only does that when leaving home. I had decided not to go to the ER two hours previously, and Wify didn't agree with that, so by bra time, there was actual fire spitting from her eyes, and she would tolerate no more crap from me. I clearly saw her putting on the bra! I stopped and doubled up for only a moment. I was moaning when I saw the magical flying clothes; my pajama pants and shirt, came at me through the air, along with booming instructions "GET DRESSED NOW! Wify be in the house! No chance now of me doing anything but exactly what she said!

Stephens County Hospital is only eight miles away through town, and I swear she covered that 15 minute drive in six minutes, running red lights and leaving flames all the way along Prather Bridge Rd.. I walked moaning into the door, grabbed a wheelchair, and sat down, rocking back and forth. By the time I wheeled myself up to the counter (only 20 feet away), Wify had parked and got there with me at ER admissions. I mentioned gut wrenching pain in lower abdomen that was radiating up into my chest. When I said chest, the gal behind the plastic heard "heart" and in short order they wheeled me back into their ER cave, and the heart monitor appeared. They got me in bed there, put nice little sticky pads on every hair they could find on my abdomen, and started turning dials. That was followed shortly by the fentanyl- two delightful doses in a couple hours I think, in the ER. That dulled PAIN only a very little, and I kept trying to tell the Dr. I needed something more. He explained the danger of stopping my heart with too much, so clearly he intended to just let PAIN do that for him. Yes, I know that is not fair to that Dr. He was trying to save me; to figure things out. Still, I was drugged and these thoughts come.

I did not think my life was in danger at that point. Not so sure in retrospect. I mean look at the stupid decisions I'd made already! Over the next six hours or so, I had an X Ray and a CAT Scan, and was prodded to death by various hands that just had to poke my stomach and lower abdomen, apparently just to hear me moan even louder. Maybe they were waiting for my friend FART to show up, but he stubbornly refused! Then the Dr. called my Stomach Surgeon in Gainesville, GA. I'd had bariatric bypass three years before, with wonderful results, and absolutely no complications, until now. My Dr. simply said, "Get him down here." Hallelujah!

I was being transported, so I was in for a delightful 60 mile drive! Just for good measure, they gave me "15 mikes" more of fentanyl just before putting me in the ambulance at 2:30 AM Saturday morning. PAIN hopped right in beside me, of course, and I'm sure I said another prayer or two along the way. I heard the ambulance guy say, "You'll be asleep in a few minutes with that last dose."

Now the only bed in the Gainesville Hospital was a double room, so Wify could not come with me. She couldn't get in the ambulance, and they don't want family visiting at 3:30 AM in double rooms—it makes sense. So I did the best thing I did that whole night—and probably one of the few correct things: I sent her home. Her other choice was a waiting room chair in the Gainesville hospital, which was nowhere near me. By that time, we'd both been awake since 7 AM the previous day, and one of the two of us would need a functioning brain the next day. That was not likely to be mine. Even with the fire spitting from her eyes, she realized the wisdom of that. She needed sleep, so she went home.

It turns out ambulance drivers can really drive, even faster than scared wives can, so we made that 60 mile trip in just under 45 minutes, I think. PAIN enjoyed every minute of that—I did not. Unfortunately, ambulance guy was wrong, and I stayed awake. Turns out PAIN can trump medicine— at least fentanyl given in 3 medical doses.

I got checked into my second ER, and my second hospital in just under eight hours (that might be a record!). Just to allow me to spend a bit more time with PAIN, I had another CAT scan, and another X Ray; more prodding hands, but then the good stuff came out, MORPHINE!

MORPHINE is my friend. I got that first dose at maybe 3:30 or 4 AM. Time was a blur by then—no real sleep, yet, just PAIN. They said I could have more at 6 AM, but "not before, so don't ask!" I watched the clock the whole time—yes, I really did stay awake for 23 hours, with much of that in the worst PAIN I've ever felt. As it turns out MORPHINE really was my friend. Six AM came with me watching the clock on the wall, and my old friend PAIN was still around, just moved aside a bit. I put off the 6 AM MORPHINE feeding but then I asked for the second dose at 7:30, because by then PAIN was coming on again pretty strong. By 8, I was talking to my Dr's surgical associate. I had my speech all planned, and all without a single curse word! I wasn't going to cuss that Dr., or any of the folks helping me. I was angry at PAIN, not those trying to help, so my planned speech held no curse words (I really remember doing none of that at all the whole night, I think. I was proud of that). After his introduction, and in my most polite moaning voice, I said:

"Good morning, Dr. I'm free in 30 minutes or so. Would you like to cut something today?"

The Dr. later laughed with me at that (I'd told him days later it was planned speech), and mentioned he'd rarely had a patient ASKED to be cut up first thing in the interview. PAIN was clearly winning, and the Dr. could tell. He'd seen the doses, the X Rays, the 2 CAT scans, etc., I should have been in coma under the table somewhere, but wasn't, and he understood gut pain fights pain relievers, including very strong ones. It took him only a few minutes or so to agree, and say "We'll start for the gut blockage laparoscopically, but I may have to cut a bit, depending on what I find in there." I then signed forms for two types of surgery, a few other things, drugs to knock me out. I signed anything, just get me under! I may have singed something to sell Trump Tower up in New York, or bought real estate in Bagdad for all I knew. I didn't care. If it was there, I signed it—just get me under fast, please!

The Dr. did mention that I have a high tolerance for PAIN: Who knew? By then, I'd lost that fight, and again, I didn't care. I just wanted to shout "Hallelujah! Cut as long as you like, Dr., but just make it stop."

Then the Dr. won me over again. I was trying to be nice when I said, "Dr. please do that later today, or as early tomorrow as you can, if you can. I've been awake since yesterday morning, and I can't do much more of this," and I meant that. I knew that PAIN can kill a human body, and I'm an old guy! That wasn't the first time I had wondered if my life could end that night, or morning or whatever. Then I said another of my very short prayers "God help me get through this." Still, the Dr. won me over again, when he said, "OH no, we're not going to wait till tomorrow."

I could have shouted with joy, even with PAIN still sitting right there in my gut and chest. Dr. said, "I'll go see what the OR schedule looks like." I could have cried—maybe I did. My thoughts, were something like "PRAISE JESUS! THANK YOU for skilled surgeons taking me seriously! And more MORPHINE, if you please!"

I'm not sure you should pray for pain killers. Maybe that first part counts for another prayer, I don't know. I did say a more serious, "Thank you" to God along about then. But at that exact moment, PAIN was joined by PANIC: It hit like a thunder clap:

MY GIRL AIN'T HERE! MY WIFY DOESN'T KNOW!

So I started doing math—my brain, those drugs, hours and hours with no sleep, but I was doing math! It was 8:30 AM and I'd been awake for 26 hours by then, maybe with a bit of slumber after MORPHINE dose one—I really don't know. Wify had been up 19 hours before I sent her home, and I figured she had to be still sleeping. I mean she'd gotten home only 6 hours previously. That couldn't be right? But it was. I didn't want to do this without Wify. I was scared, and PAIN and PANIC laughed right out loud then.

Clearly, Prayer Time. "God I am going to need help here, and please get me a phone."

Have you ever prayed for a cellphone? I hadn't, but it was a night of firsts for me. I really needed a phone—mine was 65 miles away in Toccoa. PAIN had made sure I didn't think much when the magical flying clothes came my way. Then I thought, what if her phone is off? That was the scariest thing of all.

I remember seeing a guy standing in the hallway, obviously talking with someone about a patient in another room. I thought, I could simply ask to use his phone, right? Of course, visitors give cellphones to clearly drugged up, ill patients they don't know in hospital rooms, all the time, right? Even my sleep deprived neurons figured that this idea was a non-starter.

PAIN laughed at that and then I actually heard PAIN speak; "OK Dude, 1 Ibuprophine, an Oxy for good measure, 3 doses Fentanyl, two of MORPHINE, sleep deprivation for 27 hours, and I'm still here, and your Wify ain't! I Gotcha Now!"

I'm pretty sure I cried; I clearly had a problem. But then I did something smart, I talked with the nurse. I explained that my Dr. was trying to get me into surgery—he'd heard that much--and that my Wify didn't even know about it. Turns out my problem was solved instantly. He just pulled an old phone from a drawer in his cabinet, and plugged that bad boy in: "Just dial 9 for an outside line."

Fingers didn't work just right, but after two attempts, some thirty seconds later I'm talking to WIFY. She is already steaming, hell bent for leather, my way! Sixty five miles of burning rubber, right down HWY 365! "THANK YOU, GOD!" I'm glad she didn't kill herself driving that road trip. After I hung up, I got this image of WIFY, wearing blazing silver chest armor on a giant white steed, reins in one hand and a burning sword in another, slaying all who got in her way, jumping castle walls and rivers, tearing through all creation just to get to me (I have mentioned the drugs, right? My mind was a bit loopy by then). May God bless that wonderful, wonderful, wonderful, bride of mine!

PANIC left defeated; never saw that sucker again. PAIN was still there, so I said a big SCREW YOU (actually something a bit less polite) to PAIN. With WIFY on her way, Drs. I trusted finally willing to cut my gut open, and GOD waiting for the next poor, uninspired prayer from me, it was time for me to look PAIN right in the face and say;

"Get Ready Dude! MY TEAM IS COMING FOR YOU!"

I found out later that I bounced 2 folks out of the OR, and I do feel bad about that. Still, it was protocol, and apparently my deal was that serious; By then FART had left the picture altogether—it was going to take much more than FART, no matter how inspired, no matter how memorable, to get my gut right.

I went to Pre OP, about 9:30 AM (more prayers in there), and the Nurse (Her name was Faith; I remember that I liked the Biblical name) asked about decisions that might need to be made, or advanced directives. I just pointed to WIFY and said, there she is. She makes any and all decisions. I really didn't think there would be any, but I had not made winning decisions for that last (let's see 7 AM to 7 AM, plus 3) 27 hours, and I'd had enough drugs to open my own drug store. They poked and prodded some more, and another Dr. came in and began to talk with me about putting me under.

I didn't really care about it all, but she was, of course, required to say it. Just cut to the chase, and get me my drugs—PUT ME UNDER! For me it was "Sooner is better than latter! Drugs please!" PAIN still sat right there in my gut, but WIFY was here, her beautiful eyes spitting fire, ready to do whatever was necessary. More importantly, GOD was listening.

WIFY couldn't come into the OR so she didn't see the next part. It was the cruelest PAIN of all, and it came when I was in the OR getting ready. They laid me down flat for the first time in 28 hours, and my gut ripped open—or so I thought. It felt like it exploded—and I was still praying for FART, but as I said above, FART had left the building. No new drugs yet; just PAIN, a total, complete, all consuming, gut wrenching PAIN! I'm running out of adjectives here, and that's rare for me. Still, you guys get the picture.

PAIN almost won right there! For 27 hours, I'd been in chairs or beds that allowed me to sit up a bit, or hold my legs up crossed on each other, or something other than prone. A prone position—laying down flat—gave my whole body over to PAIN. When they laid me down the gut PAIN came all the way up to my eyeballs! I remember saying, "I can't do this! I can't lay down! Put me under then lay me down, Please! Please let me sit up or cross my legs, or raise them; then poke all you want to." By then 4 nurses or op room techs, or whoever, including 2 fairly big guys, were virtually on top of me, holding me down. I remember saying, "Guys, I'm coming off this table if I don't get drugs now!" I'm not sure if I could have tossed them all off to sit up, but I was about ready to try. Then, one of them got smart and put a mask on my face! Thank you! Thank you! Thank you!

WRONG! WRONG! WRONG! Within four or five breaths I said, "Guys, this ain't working." I had thought the mask brought the drugs. WRONG! Then the biggest dude of all was in my sight, partially laying on top, and I swear he apologized to me with his eyes. What he said was, "Sorry, that's just oxygen." I knew he'd tried to trick me with the mask. He knew that I knew. I'd have done the same to keep a patient on that table. Not fair, but there it is.

Before I formulated just exactly how to cuss out that guy, I heard the Dr. behind me say, "I just got the drugs into your IV." I mumbled another, "Thank you, God." I wonder if that Dr. thought I was talking to her? I wonder if I even said that out loud.

Silence. Nothing. No PAIN.

I'd told Wify before I went under to wait and call my two brothers and my son until after the operation. She'd then have something to tell them.

Such was my drug involved thinking. She ignored me, of course, and made the calls anyway when I went in, the right choice on her part.

I don't know if this ordeal could have killed me. I think maybe yes, but I didn't ask the Dr. That probably depends on how long I ignored PAIN during those first hours. What if I'd been stubborn enough to go four hours, or five before heading to an ER? What if the bra came out of the drawer after seven hours? Would my body have taken that? My Dr. later in the week did say, "You know you waited way too long to come in, right?" I am actually humbled at how stupid I can be at times. That's what I get for ignoring WIFY. Note to self: Be smart enough to never, ever do that again.

So most of the next part, WIFY did, not me. My mind was gone; blackness. No PAIN. Like me, she was tested in this. Like me she did not falter or fail. Not my Girl! Not in any way. She can do anything. I've often told folks over the years that, if I asked her to move a mountain down to the shore, then Clingman's Dome would be on Tybee Island in a week, along with most of rest of the Smokies! She does sometimes overdo things a bit.

I learned later that about an hour into the procedure, the Dr. stopped cutting—it had become a very serious operation. He left the table and called her cell. He opened with: "We have a decision to make."

Again, my WIFY can handle a lot, a lot more than me. She will move mountains if I ask her too, but you have to admit, that sentence alone sounds a bit ominous.

Dr. said something like, "I think about half of his bowel is dead, showing no blood flow." Part of my small intestine had been removed from my direct digestive track during my gastric bypass three years ago, but it had been left in my body. It still created juices for the lower part of the digestive track, even though food did not flow through that tube. Somehow, an adhesion had grown and had now starved that bowel of its blood supply. It had died. Still, the choices were not as bad as the sentence above sounded.

Door Number ONE: Remove obviously dead portions of bowel and see if some of the other parts recover with restored blood flow. This would require me being in an induced coma for 2 or 3 days on a ventilator. They would then see what else to remove.

Door Number TWO: Get 'ur done! Get that damned dead gut out right now!

WIFY made the right call. "My husband would not want that ventilator thing. Get it out." The Dr. said he'd have made that same call if it was him, so Door Number Two it is! At that point, the one hour operation turned into about four and a half hours, so the bumped patients waited a few more hours, or days, and several other surgeons played another round of golf.

Thank you, God, for WIFY, and for her courage, and for that decision.

Saturday afternoon: big blur. I'd hit the really, really heavy post-op drugs. And then, with my mind every bit as clear as a murky, mud puddle, I awoke. It was 2:30 PM in Post OP, and I was rolled into a double room on the bariatric floor. That is where my Dr. wanted me, and another double room was all they had. PAIN was still there, but the horrid, biting gut pain was mostly gone—it was now incision pain, and some swollen gut stuff.

I remember that I texted a Gremlin (i.e. folks WIFY and I are trying to help rebuild their lives) and told her I would not be picking her up for church the next morning. I told her to get the word out to her Mom, who also needed a ride. That scared that girl to death, and that required a few more texts. As Gremlins go, she's one of the good ones.

Putting my phone down, I said Hi again to PAIN, but then I got to know Calvin, my roomy through the curtain. Calvin was my roomy for only 2 hours or so, in that double room, but in some ways, that was one of the most important parts of my stay. Calvin is 89, and his wife "went to be with the Lord," three years ago. I knew then I would like this guy when I heard him describe her death in that way. They were missionaries for years in the Philippians, and at some point he was a band director in Colorado. He and I talked for a couple hours back and forth through the curtain. He talked about his amazing life, his wife, his daughter, really intimate stuff (turns out old men who think they are facing death have no boundaries in what they might discuss). I told him about WIFY, my son, Granddaughters in Denver, my brothers, and my Gremlins. I remember telling him about a recent book I'd written for and about the Gremlins, Bible Lessons for Broken People. It's still used by some of them, even today. He said he wanted a copy, so I had WIFY bring one by the next day. Cal and I bonded in some special way, for no reason at all. I truly don't know why.

Then his daughter came in. He lives with her now, so he introduced me through the curtain. So then, I shut up for a while. A bit later, She was saying something about one of her kids that was a rather personal concern, and I said, "Calvin; Your daughter knows I'm still awake over here right? Sorry but I'm hearing all this." Then, being an ever-confident member of the Carmichael Clan, I joined in. Now, many of you guys will understand that overt family reference—think iron will, absolute confidence in our own wisdom, supreme belief in our own capabilities, and a stupid sense that we Carmichaels always understand things better than anyone else. We know that's not true, but we choose to believe it anyway!

I said to have that teenager read Philippians 4: 8. That is a beautiful passage about controlling our thoughts and focusing on noble things—the good things God gives us. That verse helps us cope when times are hard. I often have my Gremlins read that short verse.

Now being both a Carmichael, and an arm-chair psychologist, I always point out that the BIBLE is the best psychology text on the planet— the psychology within Jesus' teaching, within Paul's beautiful letters, not to mention the extensive, amassed wisdom thousands of years, in the Old Testament. The Philippians passage is God's way of telling us that by controlling our thoughts, we can control our moods, our happiness, and our behavior. By the time I'd made the recommendation to my side of the curtain, the daughter was reading the entire passage (1 – 8) on her phone, and Calvin and I said the last 4 words of it aloud with her "Think on these things." I should note that her translation on the phone was more modern, and it didn't include those last four words, but Cal knew them by heart, and we said them simultaneously. I really like that guy!

Then they came in to move me to a private room. I remember saying, "No! I don't want to! I can't leave my man, Calvin!" I think that shocked the nurse, but I was still very much "drugged" (maybe 3 or 4 hours post-op at that point), so she beautifully ignored me. Cal took it in stride: "Come back for a visit, Billy!" "I will, Cal."

I promised to come visit Cal during the rest of my stay, and I did. We didn't talk much together those few times as I strolled by in the hall over the next five days (the Drs. wanted me up and walking), and often I peeked in only to find Calvin asleep. Still, we did speak a few more times though not as intimately as before. I left him the book and my contact info. I told him that WIFY and I would take him to dinner when he got out. He said he'd like that. I do hope he calls.

"God, please bless my man, Calvin. He's one of the Good Ones! And thanks for him, and for all the good he has done, and for the life he has led. Bless Him."

Sunday afternoon comes with a couple friends from church, a Dr. in my Sunday school class, and his wife. He's another one of the good ones, and so is she. I enjoyed that visit. My Minister came on Monday, May God Bless that Man! He prayed with me and for me. My church really showed up in every way during the entire ordeal. Thank You Church, and Thank God.

And then a Gremlin came by. She wanted to surprise me with a visit! She's one of the daughters I never really had (Three of my Gremlins just call me Dad now, and I rather like it it!). She brought along Boyfriend and Baby. Very carefully, I got to hold Squirmy-K, a delightful 8 month old that I frequently babysit, to help this particular Gremlin. We visited, and they told me they loved me, and then left. Another quick prayer: "Thank you God for my new daughters, my good friends."

But then, I'm alone with FEAR: That is when FEAR really showed up. In some ways, FEAR was actually worse than PAIN.

By then, WIFY had filled me in on her decisions during the operation, and I had begun to realize what could have happened—FEAR. I had dead tissue inside of me, and nobody knows how long. The Dr. still doesn't understand how I didn't feel PAIN much, much sooner. Why didn't it come over a period of days or weeks? I had partner Drs at that point, and both were sent from God. One had given me 15 or 20 more years of life in my original bariatric surgery 3 years ago, the other—his partner had simply saved my life that Saturday morning. I told them so. Neither knew, or probably ever will, why PAIN waited so long to show up. I also had the best nurses and techs on the planet; they tolerated my sense of humor (Thank you guys! You helped save me; Thank you. Maybe one day you'll see this; Thank you).

I said again, "God help me." I've mentioned that I'm a real expert in really short prayers, and I disturb my CREATOR maybe 25 or 30 times daily, probably more this past week. I must be quite a bother to CREATOR, but I've been invited to do that; its part of the deal for a Jesus follower. I do make certain that many of the short prayers are for others, and some are just to say Thanks. They are not all merely "Billy's wish list!"

Over Sunday afternoon and Monday morning, I was still heavily medicated (some T drug in the IV that I didn't bother to remember), and Dilaudid. That's the really heavy, stuff: four times more powerful than my friend, MORPHINE. By Sunday, WIFY and I had talked out a schedule. I was in for a few days, maybe a week or longer. No reason for her to stay all day over there, with me in and out of it. I told her to just endure the drives, buy the gas, to drive slow, BUT JUST COME (65 miles house to hospital). WIFY came over each morning and evening (here's the math; 2 round trips daily, 65 miles one way, 260 miles daily).

And now the FEAR. I had Damn Near Died! Not really, but that was my FEAR. My own body had tried to kill me. How could I not know? I'm not sure any of that is true, and I really didn't want to ask, but FEAR doesn't need things to be true. FEAR only needs you to think they might be. FEAR was the enemy now. I knew the real danger had passed, the operation had been successful, the biting bowel pain was mostly gone, so why did FEAR show up then?

So I told WIFY. I remember telling her Monday morning that I was getting depressed, and maybe scared. PAIN was still there; Incision Pain, and swollen bowel pain. I had seven to ten days of PAIN left, just in the hospital, and to be sure, PAIN was waiting for me at home after that! For now, I had Dilaudid in a self-administered rig, but PAIN was still there.

After Wify's Monday morning visit, FEAR really got to me. I think I may have been shaking but I'll be damned if I was going to push that Dilaudid button! It wasn't biting PAIN: it was FEAR of future PAIN I was feeling. I didn't want that to go on, but I didn't have any say in the matter. Again, a quick prayer; "God help me. Sorry, but I really do need you this time."

No burning bush; no column of flame or wind of the Holy Spirit. Just me saying silently, or maybe out loud; "God, I really need you!"

I'm like most poor creatures on this planet; I often pray, but I really only "cry out" to God, once in a long, long while. That's when I have nothing left. I was there, at that place, for a while emotionally, and I was really, really scared. My Gremlins will understand that; they live there, may God bless each and every one of them.

Amazingly, CREATOR doesn't mind my crying out at all. Maybe it's my killer sense of humor, but I view her (or him) sitting up there somewhere, amid the usual planet house-keeping duties, and the billions of prayers headed her way, hearing me/hearing that prayer from someone who is really scared. He'd laugh a bit to himself, and then said something like,

"AH, I see I finally have Billy Bender's attention! My, but that boy is stubborn! I've got hold of a real Carmichael, here."

So that is when God showed up again, and HE TOUCHED ME. He showed up and TOUCHED ME! Of course, some might say, "Drug induced imaginings" or "Results of trauma." Let them say those things. They are not wrong, they are just incomplete somehow. I know God and God knows me; He touched me. He knows me by name, and that's just really, really cool. He knows you by name too; You should check that out: Isaiah 43: 1.

God was there, right there with me, and right there for me. He showed up in an old song. I remember thinking, I believe (I think I was going to say in God, or I believe in you Jesus, or who knows), but SONG took over.

I believe (I paused just a bit, and the melody and words came into my mind),

In a hill called Mt. Calvary.

I believe whatever the cost.

And when time has surrendered, and life is no more,

I'll still cling to that old rugged cross.

SONG showed up from nowhere! I hadn't been singing; didn't think I was going to. Strange, but there it is. SONG just showed up; my burning bush.

A problem here though: the thing is, the miracle here is this: I don't know that song! I remember it and I knew the tune but not the words. I don't know any of the verses and I'm not sure even today, if that chorus is accurate in wording, but that's what came to my mind. That's what I saw, and felt, and experienced somehow. SONG overtook me. I could not stop humming it, so I often just sang it. Since then several folks have said they'ed look it up, and get the real words, if these are not accurate, but I told them not too. Maybe at some point, but not now. What I had now, were the lines that flooded into my mind then, those lines above, and a rich, beautiful melody. So after 70 years, right in the in the middle of FEAR, my burning

bush just showed up. I am his, and he is mine. THANK YOU, CREATOR.
THANK YOU, JESUS.

Now I really need to make this clear. My Mom, long ago passed, played
the piano in church since before I can remember. I grew up with her playing
those old beautiful hymns at home and church, and many, many of them
touch me in special ways, even today. I'll always love the old hymns with a
passion. I know many by heart, 3 or 4 verses and beautiful, rich choruses.
Wonderful statements of faith. God's Treasures.

Just As I Am Without One Plea--I walked down a church aisle to that
one, when I was in grade 5, and most certainly I was in the wrong church!
That's another story for another day.

The Old Rugged Cross, I Come to the Garden Alone, He Lives!, Alas
and Did my Savior Bleed, and of course the three "Holy Positions"—
Leaning, Standing, and Love Lifted me.

Now I get how Standing on the Promises, is a bodily position, along
with Leaning on the Everlasting Arms, but Love? Why did that old joke
from my childhood talking about 3 holy Positions include Love as one?
Is Love a position: a stance toward God maybe? Again, another story for
another time.

I could, and often do, sing those old hymns, riding alone in my car, or
just sitting in a chair at home. I feel like I'm giving worship to God (in the
Bible it says it—make a joyful noise), and I can sing them all from memory,
anytime (just ask), at least the first and last verse. So why does my burning
bush turn out to be a song I don't really know, beyond a few lines of the
chorus? Lines I'm really not sure of? The hand of God is in there somewhere.

Well, we really are here as God's creatures—his little animated
cartoons; we are his breath, his choice, his expression of himself, as a life
in the universe. We are her (or his) pleasure, at least when we are at our
best. Anyway, I like to think he will sometimes playfully rag us out a bit.
We are God's blessed amusement, and that often involves play. You see, in

my relationship with WIFY, and both of my Brothers, and My Son—the closest, most dear relationships in my life, we do love to play, to "Pick on" each other a bit, or nag each other some. That is playful love. The humor in those relationships IS part of the love. My older brother Jack and I do that most of all, but Willie (my son) ain't at all bad at this, and Wade, (my kid brother), He has the best sense of humor of all. In those dear relationships, the humor is the love.

Maybe CREATOR just thought using that old song that I didn't know was funny. I don't know. It may be merely another way to make me look up and learn a new song. I'll do that, but not yet.

So my column of fire, my burning bush is a partially remembered chorus of an old song that I don't know. Still, it came when I could take no more, and it saved me; With that song, CREATOR saved me. Now it reminds me of my priorities. Now it took a while, over the next two days to get there; to reach that insight. It was not immediate. Still every time I felt that tune come on (and it did very often during my six days in the hospital), I'd sing that chorus. Nurses must have heard me some; I don't know, or care. I'd sing it alone in my room, and they would come and go as needed (Thanks to all those Nurses and techs! You guys helped save me no less than my Drs.; Thank you). Night and day I'd sing, sometimes over and over again.

In the next days, I'd share that song and that bit of this story with other Jesus followers. Like I said, my church really stepped up. My "Young Gent's Coffee Association" (Tuesday morning coffee group, we ain't gentlemen and we sure ain't young!)—was texting me in my drug induced haze by the second morning! Thanks Guys. And thanks to those others of you who visited, or texted, or texted WIFY. May God Bless You. I told my brother Jack some of this, but I'm not sure I communicated this part—the most important part, of this story well.

The song made me see things; GOD had saved me, CREATOR had chosen to save me this time! He saved me from gut tearing PAIN, from PANIC, from FEAR, maybe from death. I really was scared of that, but now somehow, I think that even if I had died, it would have been OK. Had that happened, it would be CREATOR'S will. It would have made very little difference to me because I'd then be with CREATOR. I feel like maybe I can do death now. I think I understand how, now, I think.

I think that, if we are lucky, we all hit that realization, that maybe we really can deal with our own death. This then, is when you become immortal. But maybe a better way to say that is, you realize you already ARE immortal. CREATOR made you immortal. We all have death in our future, and if we are Jesus Followers, we'll be with Jesus and CREATOR. Maybe there is no good way to say that—no expression sufficient that, for CREATOR'S gifts to us, our joyfully temporary life, our humor, our redemption, a questioning mind, Jesus, our families, our churches; these are CREATOR'S gifts to us. These show CREATOR'S LOVE.

And there it is: CREATOR'S LOVE.   GOD'S LOVE.

His love of me, of WIFY, of the Doctors, nurses, techs and all who saved me. His love of Cal. His love for you and all his other creatures; his love for all his creation.

It is all about CREATOR'S LOVE. There is nothing else, nothing else of importance. That's the best prayer of all. "CREATOR: Thank you for your LOVE. AMEN."

Still, SONG kept coming back, so I'd sing it or hum it again.

I believe in a hill called Mt. Calvary.

I believe whatever the cost.

And when time has surrendered, and life is no more,

I'll still cling to that old rugged cross.

I had a running debate, and would sometimes switch the words life and time in line 3. Don't know which is right, if either is. For me it worked both ways. SONG had arrived; Burning bush was here. God was with me.

OK: You might say, Drug induced emotions? FEAR subsiding? PAIN reaction? Or The Touch of God. None of those are inaccurate. It's up to you to pick one, I guess, if you must. Maybe pick all of the above? I don't have to convince anyone of anything. At this point, it's just my job to tell this story. That is who I am; who God made me to be. I write, I tell stories. It's similar to WIFY and my work with Gremlins. My job to get them in the door of God's house. God always takes care of the rest. Now don't get me wrong. We buy Bibles by the train load, along with computers and quite a few cars only to give them away to Gremlins. We do hours of discussions and Bible reading with these folks; we're always talking about Jesus with them, and I bore them to death inviting them to church—particular my 3 new daughters. One was recently baptized, and another recently "walked the long walk" down that aisle and joined our church. Still, in all, WIFY and I are only information sources, poor examples of what we should be, maybe we help with transportation a bit. CREATOR handles the heavy lifting, the conviction.

Still, given the choices above? Well, for me there is no doubt. GOD TOUCHED ME. CREATOR'S LOVE TOUCHED ME! And right there, another old song line comes to mind. "He touched me, and made me whole." "Thank you again, God for these beautiful rich treasures, these wonderful old hymns, and memories of my Mom playing them."

I wonder why God didn't use that song with me. I mean at least I know that song. Now some ten days later (it's now Monday) I think I hear him/ her smiling, even as I write that sentence. Turns out CREATOR is full of surprises.

That's it, then. SONG —my SONG—would show up, and I'd sing that hymn. In some way, my burning bush became SONG, and then became a sign of CREATOR'S LOVE.

Once many years ago I traveled to Jerusalem, and I actually touched Calvary. Still, SONG means so much more to me, than that memory of actually being there; strange. At this point, SONG--that hill on Mt.

Calvary-- has become a prayer of thanks for me. I've told WIFY to respect my use of that SONG as a prayer of thanks. I must have sang it 20 or 30 times a day. I was healing; I am still healing. SONG helps. PAIN, PANIC, FEAR, all gone, now.

As it turns out, PAIN, is really just a warning that I should have listened to much sooner; its gone now. Now, I have a delightful 9 inch scar, and 26 staples (still with me!). But most important, I have a new assurance of CREATOR'S LOVE. I have been blessed by all this.

I hope, and I pray that maybe you have too.

REFLECTION 32:

So Where Are We Now?

H aving been non-political for about a month as God worked on my growth, it's past time for a few political thoughts on this 2/11/24. I had thought that the original *Diary of a Deplorable*, would end with Reflection Number 30, but I think now that I have to add Reflections 31 and 32. The book has been accepted for publication by a vanity press, and should be published by election time, this fall. With that in mind, here's a new "culmination."

Biden is still a demented, barely functional old guy. However, one thing changed last week. Now, even his own administration is admitting that! Just last week (early February, 2024) a report came out from the Special Prosecutor appointed by slow joe's department of injustice. That report investigated biden's bumbling, in handling highly classified documents. As you might recall, Trump's house was raided by the FBI in a dark-of-night, terror raid, similar to the Gestapo tactics of Hitler's Germany. Trump has now been indicted and is facing charges.

Of course, we now know that slow joe did exactly the same "crime," but as noted before, damocrats, blacks, and liberals get a pass when they break the law. The report concluded that while slow joe had willfully broken the law, he was not to be prosecuted, because of his age, and his failing memory! That report questioned his mental faculties noting his age, and his incapacity to understand things. It pointed out that prosecution of someone with his mental faculties would be impossible! In fact, during the same week the report came out, slow joe discussed meeting recently with a French President, who has unfortunately, been dead since 1996. He also stated that Gaza was bordering on Mexico. His mental slips are apparent to all. This is a demented mind, folks, and any honest person has to admit that. Of course few damocrats are honest about it.

Still, here's the idiocy of this farce. If biden's mental faculties and memory are so bad he cannot be held to the same legal standard as Trump and everyone else, then why should even damocrats believe that his memory and metal faculties are sufficient to serve another four years as President, as leader of the free world? Such a position is simply stupidity! Further, since the report came out, even damocrats are beginning to think about replacing slow joe as the next democratic presidential nominee.

Now, as stated before in the Diary, many of us believe that this biden presidency, has merely been a third obummer term in office. Obummer has often demonstrated his hatred of American Exceptionalism, and only someone who truly hates America could have done the things that slow joe's administration has done. These include leaving the southern border open to invasion by over 6 million persons, including many thousands of men of military age, an assortment of MS 13 members, hundreds of known terrorists, and drug mules carrying a nice assortment of illegal drugs, fostering multiple wars, allowing China to run wild, and allowing Putin to grab more land in Europe. When we add to that the ill-preparedness of the American military—a military stressing proper use of self-selected pronouns rather than defense of the greatest nation on earth, we see in the harsh light of reality the poor state of America. All of this weakens America, and one has to assume that this weakening is intentional. Again, I and many others believe obummer has been pulling the strings, and we should add that his was the first administration in recent memory to weaponize the agencies of the federal government against conservative Christians.

I recently watched a movie called 2000 Mules. It was another piece of hard evidence that the 2020 Presidential election was stolen, based on *improper handling of millions of ballots by "mules" who stuffed ballots from God Knows Where into ballot drop boxes in five different highly democratic districts in swing states—the very states that gave the election to slow jow.*

As the evidence mounts that the 2020 election was, in fact, a coup, more and more of us are becoming aware that the same thing could happen in 2024—Trump is now winning by a fairly wide margin in almost all of the polls—from 5 to 10 percent, so if that remains the same, he should be our next President. That is my prayer—that he will win, and once again save this nation from the horror of the damocrats. However, damocrats have cheated on elections before (read 2020) and they still have the funding to hire the same 2000 mules.

Around the world, things continue to go as one might expect, with slow joe in the White House. American influence is waning across the globe, China is preparing for war with the US, while the US is not, and once China decides to grab Taiwan, things will heat up fairly quickly. If China is smart (and they are), they will do that prior to the Presidential election, while slow joe (read obummer) still controls power. Recall that obummer simply let Putin take hunks of land during his administration, and there is no reason to assume that China's stealing of Taiwan would be met with anything other than a placid shoulder shrug from obummer, and a few babbled incoherent words from slow joe.

We must also note that talk of civil war in America is heading up. The state of Texas has decided to defend it's own border and stop illegal immigration, and they are now beginning to quarrel with the feds. Texas has mobilized it's National Guard troops to block sections of the southern border, within the last month, and slow joe's homeland insecurity office is objecting! Several other states have sent their state forces (Florida National Guard is one example) to assist Texas. Can this lead to an actual Civil War? One may only guess.

So here we are.

Is America doomed? Possibly.

Is America headed into a Civil War? Again, possibly.

What can we, as Conservative Christians do?

We pray, and as I said before, here is my prayer, from now through the ages: Here is my burning bush.

I believe in a hill called Mt. Calvary.

I believe whatever the cost.

And when time has surrendered, and life is no more,

I'll still cling to that old rugged cross.

As Christians, We pray, we stand for liberty, and we gently, quietly, stand up to tyranny. We strip the damocrats bear of their pig-headed dishonesties, and we hold to Jesus as our guide, our help, our savior, and our friend.

As Paul once said, we stand for truth, and the truth shall set us free! So from one deplorable to another, I wish you all GodSpeed,

Billy